THE GOLD THIEVES

Borgo Press Books by ALEXANDRE DUMAS

Anthony
The Barricade at Clichy; or, The Fall of Napoleon
Bathilda
Caligula
The Corsican Brothers (with Eugène Grangé & Xavier de Montépin)
The Count of Monte Cristo, Part One: The Betrayal of Edmond Dantès
The Count of Monte Cristo, Part Two: The Resurrection of Edmond Dantès
The Count of Monte Cristo, Part Three: The Rise of Monte Cristo
The Count of Monte Cristo, Part Four: The Revenge of Monte Cristo
A Fairy Tale (with Adolphe de Leuven and Léon Lhérie)
The Gold Thieves (with Countess Céleste de Chabrillan)
Kean
The Last of the Three Musketeers; or, The Prisoner of the Bastille (Musketeers #3)
Lorenzino
The Mohicans of Paris
Napoléon Bonaparte
Queen Margot
Richard Darlington (with Prosper Dinaux)
Sylvandire
The Three Musketeers (Musketeers #1)
The Three Musketeers—Twenty Years Later (Musketeers #2)
The Tower of Nesle (with Frédéric Gaillardet)
The Two Dianas (with Paul Meurice)
Urbain Grandier and the Devils of Loudon
The Venetian
The Whites and the Blues
The Widow's Husband; and, Porthos in Search of an Outfit
Young Louix XIV

RELATED DRAMAS:

The Queen's Necklace, by Pierre Decourcelle
The Seed of the Musketeers, by Paul de Kock & Guénée (Musketeers #5)
The San Felice, by Maurice Drack
The Son of Porthos the Musketeer, by Émile Blavet (Musketeers #4)
A Summer Night's Dream, Adolphe de Leuven & Joseph-Bernard Rosier
The Widow's Husband; and, Porthos in Search of an Outfit: Two Dumasian Comedies, edited by Frank J. Morlock

THE GOLD THIEVES

A PLAY IN FIVE ACTS

ALEXANDRE DUMAS

And the Countess Céleste de Chabrillan

Translated and Adapted by Frank J. Morlock

THE BORGO PRESS
MMXII

THE GOLD THIEVES

Copyright © 2001, 2012 by Frank J. Morlock

FIRST BORGO PRESS EDITION

Published by Wildside Press LLC

www.wildsidebooks.com

DEDICATION

To my dear friend, Mala Belli,
for many years of friendship.

CONTENTS

CAST OF CHARACTERS	9
PROLOGUE	11
ACT I	45
ACT II	82
ACT III	123
ACT IV	152
ACT V	193
ABOUT THE AUTHOR	221

CAST OF CHARACTERS

Tom Cooper

Williams (25 years old)

Max Fulton

Doctor Ivans (50 years old)

Paul (the Marquis)

Joanne

The Parisian

Mobile

Le Faucheux

Melida

Albert

Mother Joseph

Émeraude

Louisa

Jenny

Catalin

Patrick (30 years old)

Robinson (60 years old, merchant)

PROLOGUE

A salon in Doctor Ivan's home in Portsmouth.

At rise, Louisa is alone, preparing.

LOUISA

(looking at the clock)

Four o'clock. The offices close at 4:15. Mr. Williams will be here at 4:30.

(rapping)

Good, that's the doctor knocking.

(she goes to open. Knocking in the English manner—four or five rapid taps which increase)

DOCTOR

A man didn't come here in my absence?

LOUISA

With a word from you, Doctor, allowing him to visit the house?

DOCTOR

Exactly.

LOUISA

Oh—sir—what's he come to do here? He looked and inventoried all the furniture as if he were going to buy them.

DOCTOR

He came precisely for that. Did he speak to the ladies?

LOUISA

Only to Miss Émeraude.

DOCTOR

Fine. Where is he?

LOUISA

He must be in your office now.

DOCTOR

My poor furniture. Each of them brings back a memory.

(Patrick enters and looks at him.)

DOCTOR

What are you doing here?

PATRICK

Me? Nothing, sir. I was coming in to help Miss Louisa prepare the tea. If you have orders for me—

DOCTOR

Have you prepared your accounts?

PATRICK

Then the Doctor is sending me away?

DOCTOR

On the contrary, it's you who are sending us away since you don't wish to come with us.

PATRICK

You didn't give me time to think it over, sir.

DOCTOR

(low to Louisa)

Are they busy packing?

LOUISA

The ladies have done nothing else all day.

DOCTOR

And with what mood?

LOUISA

Miss Melida was sad; Miss Émeraude was joyful.

DOCTOR

Poor Melida—but it has to be done. I'm going to my office, if the ladies ask after me, you will say I've returned but that I am busy.

LOUISA

Yes, doctor.

(He leaves, sighing.)

PATRICK

Ah—then—so it's decided—completely decided?

LOUISA

What?

PATRICK

The departure.

LOUISA

You can see plainly since the Doctor told you to deliver your accounts to him.

PATRICK

Well—and you?

LOUISA

And me—what?

PATRICK

You're leaving, too?

LOUISA

Doubtless.

PATRICK

You're going to expatriate yourself—?

LOUISA

I'll follow my mistress.

PATRICK

You will follow your mistress—that's well said that is.

LOUISA

Is it not the duty of a good servant to follow their masters?

PATRICK

Doubtless when the change of residence is reasonable; but when the master's change residence to go establish themselves in the Antipodes, that's another matter. Do you know where these Antipodes are, Miss Louisa?

LOUISA

No.

PATRICK

Well, I've informed myself about it. It's exactly 3,000 leagues beneath my feet—directly—in a country where men walk with their heads down and their feet in the air—where day is night and night is day—where they burn in winter and freeze in summer—Come on! Does one go to such an unreasonable country?

LOUISA

Apparently since we are going there.

PATRICK

But you'll never come back from there.

LOUISA

Then say your goodbyes to me.

PATRICK

What! Goodbye—

LOUISA

Yes—goodbye.

PATRICK

Anyway, you aren't going tomorrow.

LOUISA

Who knows?

PATRICK

And you are telling me all this for true,— plainly?

LOUISA

Without any doubt.

PATRICK

Why there's a way to kill a man on the spot.

LOUISA

Bah! You will do as Mr. Williams, you will resign yourself.

PATRICK

Mr. Williams resigned! Why that means that he's like me—not quite like me—he's in despair.

LOUISA

Ah! Now there's someone who, if he were free to come as you are, wouldn't beg—he doesn't compromise with those he loves.

PATRICK

Excuse me, I seldom compromise with those I don't love—and I have my reasons for that—if you were to know.

LOUISA

I ask nothing better.

PATRICK

Have you ever made a crossing—you who speak?

LOUISA

Never—

PATRICK

Well—as for me, I made one—not very long—from Dover to Calais—I am only telling you that—and yet I am a man—!

LOUISA

A bad sailor, that's all.

PATRICK

Ah, yes—I am subject to attacks of giddiness, only looking at waves; I prefer turf to the sea; earthquakes are rare unlike big boats bearing immigrants where it's a perpetual uproar! The wind blows, the ropes screech, the boards crack, everyone is complaining—and when the weather is calm—you see them following you opening their jaws to swallow the boat! I get ill just to think of it—I was at the point that if I could do without fog, I'd never go back to England. But what do you want? I'm a true Englishman, I cannot do without fog—that's what make us so gay.

LOUISA

Well—don't leave your fog—and wish me bon voyage. Hey, someone's knocking.

PATRICK

I hear, I hear.

LOUISA

Then go open.

PATRICK

Fine! Why rush? You can plainly hear—it's some common person—the knock of a servant probably—

LOUISA

Perhaps the one rapping so humbly is coming to seek help for some poor sick person or some injured worker! You know Doctor Ivans' orders are to open quickly—whatever may be the manner of the person knocking.

(two small knocks)

Go ahead, Patrick, go ahead!

(Patrick heads out.)

PATRICK

Coming—ah, I don't know if it's the sorrow of leaving you or the memory of the sea—but I don't feel well.

(Exit Patrick.)

LOUISA

I'm beginning to think it's really lucky I'm leaving. I might have been mad enough to marry that boy—I'd noticed he had no wit, but now I begin to see he has no heart.

(Enter Robinson with the Doctor.)

ROBINSON

Word of honor—of an honest man, Doctor Ivans, I cannot give you more than 200 pounds sterling for all this.

DOCTOR

(aside)

He ought to say—word of a trickster.

(aloud)

Anyway, can I have the money tonight by ten o'clock?

ROBINSON

I need to prepare a bill of sale.

DOCTOR

That's very true—but it will be ready in twenty minutes. Send it to me.

ROBINSON

The Bill, together with 200 pounds will be delivered to you by six o'clock, Dr. Ivans.

DOCTOR

You always have to be careful about people who give their word about everything.

(noticing the Parisian in the antechamber)

Ah! Ah! There's someone waiting for me in the antechamber, and you didn't tell me about him, Louisa?

LOUISA

I didn't know it, sir. It's that imbecile of a Patrick; he is so upset about our departure that under the pretext of helping me, he messes up everything.

DOCTOR

It's to me you wish to speak, young man?

PARISIAN

Yes, Doctor, with your permission, if it doesn't disturb you.

DOCTOR

Not in the least. Come in: I am yours.

(to Mr. Robinson)

So, at six o'clock, Mr. Robinson?

(The Parisian enters.)

ROBINSON

At six.

(He leaves.)

LOUISA

Should I tell Miss Melida to come make tea?

DOCTOR

If you like.

(Louisa leaves.)

DOCTOR

The two of us now.

PARISIAN

The honor is mine, Doctor.

DOCTOR

Look—what do you want with me?

PARISIAN

By God, you know quite well what I want with you.

DOCTOR

No—Devil take me!

PARISIAN

Oh—indeed yes! I am coming to ask a service of you—no one ever comes to you for anything else.

DOCTOR

Ah! Ah! It seems to me that I know you.

PARISIAN

I should think so, I am a patient.

DOCTOR

I treated you?

PARISIAN

And gallantly! Meaning that if I am sure of my legs, and if I have the honor of telling you, your very humble servant, Doctor Ivans—I owe it to you.

DOCTOR

Can't you be more precise?

PARISIAN

Don't you recall a drowning case, a man already green like a meadow that you, as they say—into whose lungs you breathed air, and into his esophagus you poured a little cup of Brandy.

DOCTOR

I remember. You'd thrown yourself into the sea to save a poor devil who was drowning.

PARISIAN

Go on!

DOCTOR

And you almost drowned with him.

PARISIAN

What do you want? One has heart or done doesn't. And indeed, it's a shame to a man with heart to see another drinking a cup without throwing himself in the water to drink with him.

DOCTOR

(laughing, getting up)

And you were drinking so well that without me, you would have swallowed all the water in the port of Portsmouth.

PARISIAN

Luckily you arrived; as you said: Enough like this: Let's stop the trouble and here I am.

DOCTOR

It's an old story. What do you want from me?

PARISIAN

Oh, don't worry. It's not to pay you for your prescription. What I want, since that day—I don't know if it's because I was too soaked, but my pockets are dry—you see, which is a pity—what I want—damn—it's hard to say.

DOCTOR

(putting his hand in his pocket)

Look—say it all the same.

PARISIAN

They say you are embarking for Australia.

DOCTOR

It's true.

PARISIAN

On the *Marco Polo*.

DOCTOR

That's true, too.

PARISIAN

As ship's doctor.

DOCTOR

As ship's doctor.

PARISIAN

Well—I said this to myself—Parisian, my lad—you want to see the world, but cannot pay the transportation expenses—you have to go find Doctor Ivans—he has a good heart, a man like no other—indeed! He will get you free passage. And you—during the voyage will serve him—gratis, of course. Damn—if the thing is agreeable to you, Doctor, you will be doing me a proud service.

DOCTOR

That would make you really happy?

PARISIAN

More than your refusal would cause me sorrow.

DOCTOR

Well, my friend, that works with me.

PARISIAN

Really true?

(Melida enters and concerns herself with the tea.)

PARISIAN

Ah! Doctor—if I were a crazy woman, I would kiss you—

(offering his hand)

Ah—Doctor—

(withdrawing his hand)

Pardon—pardon!

DOCTOR

Well—what?

(offering his hand)

PARISIAN

(hiding his hand behind his back)

Never! Never! Never!

DOCTOR

It's to see if you have fever.

PARISIAN

In that case it's another matter. Oh, yes—I have a fever—of joy—of—well—what are you putting in my hand, Doctor?

DOCTOR

Me? Nothing.

PARISIAN

A half crown. No—thanks—no—no!

DOCTOR

My friend, it's to drink my health—and of this child and her sister.

PARISIAN

Really—it's for that?

DOCTOR

Oh, my God, yes—! Not for anything else.

PARISIAN

If it's for that, it's sacred—and it will be done—conscientiously. By the way—when do we leave?

DOCTOR

Hush! Be here at eight o'clock in the evening—with your baggage—you will pass for one of the household.

PARISIAN

What? It's for tonight.

DOCTOR

Hush! I tell you.

PARISIAN

Ah—I understand. They don't know this yet in the family. Mum's the word, Doctor, till tonight.

DOCTOR

Till tonight, my lad.

(Exit the Parisian.)

MELIDA

There you are, Father, we've hardly seen you since morning.

DOCTOR

(looking at her)

Yes, and poor child, you've profited by my absence—to weep.

MELIDA

It's not my fault, Father. I am doing what I can! You see my mouth is smiling.

DOCTOR

(pulling out his handkerchief and drying her eyes)

Yes—and your eyes are weeping.

MELIDA

Oh—it's not for only for me! To follow you, to serve you, to love you everywhere, somewhere—that would be too much joy—! But Williams, Williams, father—

(Williams enters.)

DOCTOR

Williams is a man, my child.

MELIDA

Oh—he'll die of it—

DOCTOR

(turning and noticing Williams)

No—come tell her that, Williams—come tell her that one doesn't die for some years of absence—come tell her that hearts truly united always end by being rejoined. Come!

MELIDA

Oh—father—

DOCTOR

Console her—sustain her—be strong, Williams. Tell her I'm getting old—my child—that I have perhaps five or six years—— not more to live. God doesn't want to take me so soon from two children who have only me in the world and love me so much— but to exercise my profession. Tell her that it's necessary for me to amass down there in five or six years a little fortune that despite the trouble I took, I haven't been able to realize here. Tell her that the situation you occupy which pay 125 pounds per year doesn't suffice to support a wife and children—tell her all this, Williams—words that passing from your mouth will have greater force than coming from mine.

BOTH

Father.

DOCTOR

I know that I'm dealing with two valiant souls—two honest hearts, and that I leave them supporting each other, certain that instead of weakening, they will strengthen each other.

(He looks at them, places Melida's arm in Williams'—and leaves)

MELIDA

Williams!

(Melida falls in an armchair)

WILLIAMS

Why he thinks I have a heart of bronze—your father—

(with agitation)

Oh! My duty, I know quite well will be to sustain you—by repeating to you, word for word, the statements he just made—but I haven't the strength. I haven't the courage—this departure is killing me! Oh—the sea, the ocean—space—and you down there without me.

MELIDA

Who would heave said, Williams, that it would be I who was consoling you!

WILLIAMS

Don't try, Melida, for if you resign yourself like this, I will believe you are indifferent.

MELIDA

We will return.

WILLIAMS

You will return? And do you know that the crossing alone takes five months? Do you think that during those five months I will have a moment's rest? The noise of the wind alone will drive me mad! I don't wish to exhort you to disobedience—I love your father as if he were my own—but I feel that he's committing a folly—! And I am all the more wretched that I cannot tell him stop! He will accuse me of egoism. Poverty imposes silence on me. But if you leave, Melida—a presentment tells me that we will never see each other again.

MELIDA

(rising and crossing in front of Williams)

Why terrify me so? Why take from me my only last hope?

WILLIAMS

Because I see with the eyes of my heart! Because the ocean brought misfortune to the only being I loved as much as you—my mother—because it swallowed her without leaving me a tomb to weep over! Nothing returns from what it swallows—its depths are abysses. It's twelve years since parting with her to rejoin my father at the Cape of Good Hope. I saw my mother die. It was twelve years ago I saw a porthole open and the bier which shut in the being who loved me most in the world slide into the ocean! I saw that coffin come to the surface of the water and float on the surface in the wake of the ship, as if the dear creature didn't want to abandon me—! This terrible spectacle is not only present in my thoughts, but still before my eyes—as if it happened yesterday. When I think that you are going to cross the ocean—the same image comes before my eyes—! Oh, my God! You won't permit Melida to leave or you will grant me the favor of leaving with her.

MELIDA

Oh—if that could be—with what joy would I leave England!

WILLIAMS

Do you speak truly, Melida?

MELIDA

I swear that with you, for me all would be joy, happiness, hope.

WILLIAMS

(kissing her hand)

Melida! Well!

MELIDA

What?

WILLIAMS

I don't dare say anything—I don't dare promise you—I don't dare hope anything—but this evening at ten o'clock—expect me—and if God looks on our side—I will have good news to tell you.

MELIDA

Well what?

WILLIAMS

Nothing, nothing—for it requires a miracle.

MELIDA

I will expect you—

WILLIAMS

Goodbye—

MELIDA

Already!

WILLIAMS

It's necessary—till tonight—till tonight!

(Exit Williams.)

MELIDA

(alone)

How easily the heart hopes for what it wishes—I know nothing and I think all is possible—to escape the sorrow of a separation—

(The Doctor and Émeraude enter. The Doctor goes to sit at the table. Émeraude approaches Melida from behind and embraces her.)

MELIDA

(throwing her arms around Émeraude's neck)

Oh, Sister! Sister!

ÉMERAUDE

Silence! Our father is there.

MELIDA

My God!

ÉMERAUDE

Courage, Melida.

MELIDA

That's easy for you to say—your heart is free.

ÉMERAUDE

Free! Heavens, read this—I received that an hour ago.

MELIDA

A letter?

ÉMERAUDE

Read—

MELIDA

(reading)

"You are going to leave, Émeraude, you cannot refuse me a few minutes meeting. I am allowing myself to be sacrificed and I am so miserable for having lost you—that you must take pity on me. My name alone belongs to another—but my soul is yours and you are carrying it off with you—Sir Edward!"

ÉMERAUDE

Yes!

MELIDA

You love him?

ÉMERAUDE

As you love Williams.

MELIDA

And he is married!

ÉMERAUDE

I was poor! You see that. It's possible to be more miserable then you. You, at least, still have hope.

MELIDA

Ah—that's why you are so happy to leave?

ÉMERAUDE

I distrust myself and we need nothing less than an ocean between him and me to reassure me.

MELIDA

You are right, Émeraude. We must leave.

DOCTOR

What are you talking about over there?

MELIDA

Father, we were saying that you are supremely wise and that we will leave on the day and hour you choose.

DOCTOR

You are two brave children. You've understood, I haven't much courage and you each bring me a little of your own. Here, what future would you have, dear daughters of my heart, if death were to suddenly strike me? Alas, our society is careless with regard to young and beautiful orphans.

ÉMERAUDE

You've given us skills that we should be able to utilize if you'd allowed us.

DOCTOR

You would be governesses. Governesses! That is to say—the first servants of the house. Sacrificial lambs to all the bad humors of an aristocratic family; slaves of pupils who are deemed to obey you. I've seen many of those poor young girls; with pale faces, humble voices, eyes red with tears—all were wretched because those who employed them only had the power of money over them—the most insolent of powers.

(crossing the stage)

MELIDA

Father—human experience teaches us we are in this world to suffer.

DOCTOR

Yes, but the heart that loves you refuses to listen to that voice—or at least to believe it. Suffer, you may, poor children, that I've brooded over for twenty, twenty watchful years! My poor chicks that a mother doesn't shelter. Well—no, I rebel against human experience; to that voice which shouts misfortune, I answer: You lie! You won't suffer. As for me, I don't wish you to suffer! We shall go down under. All the papers agree in saying that doctors are needed in Australia. I'll make a fortune there. I have the credulity of people who desire and hope—when we are rich, we'll bring Williams—that's for you, Melida. As for you, Émeraude, we will find you a man of heart in need of a sweet, wise, loving wife who will give you joy—happiness—my beautiful gem.

ÉMERAUDE

Beautiful dreams—father.

DOCTOR

Which will become realities. Leave it to me—well, my good children, now that you are really reasonable, there's no reason to keep a secret from you—especially this secret—as the hour has come that I can no longer hide it.

(coming forward)

We are leaving tonight.

MELIDA

My God!

ÉMERAUDE

Oh—so much the better—father.

MELIDA

Ah—Williams.

DOCTOR

Isn't it better for you not to see him again? Don't you think those last goodbyes will be more painful than comforters?

MELIDA

Yes, yes—perhaps you're right, father. Is it permitted that I write him that I was unaware of your decision—and that it was only at the moment of leaving that I learned—

DOCTOR

Yes, write him—pour your heart in his, poor child! It's an honest heart.

(to Louisa)

Well—what is it?

(moving forward)

LOUISA

A gentleman coming on behalf of Mr. Robinson with a paper to be signed and a bag of money. I made him wait in your office.

DOCTOR

(to Louisa)

Well—bring down the trunks and the boxes—Émeraude will help you—courage my child.

MELIDA

You see plainly that I have courage, father.

(aside)

Ah, if the test were to last much longer it would kill me.

(the doctor goes into his office)

ÉMERAUDE

Courage, sister, God is watching us—Williams loves you—what are 5,000 leagues to a bird seeking spring—to a heart seeking love?

(Exit Émeraude.)

MELIDA

(alone)

Poor Williams! What's he going to say when he comes this evening and finds the house empty?

(sitting at a table and taking up a pen)

Write then, trembling hand, and if tears cloud your eyes, it's just one sorrow the more.

(writing)

"Dear Williams—fate subjects us sometimes to such cruel trials that one must squeeze up one's courage in a great love like mine so as not to die; In, an hour, I'll have left this house without seeing you again—the cradle of our love—the tomb of my hopes—my unhappiness is so great that I dare not look you in the face—if I knew I'd never see you again, I'd let myself die—but no—you will come rejoin me; very soon, right? God will take pity on those who never offended him. I love you. I love you."

(she rings—raising hear head and perceiving Patrick)

You're staying, right, Patrick?

PATRICK

Yes, Miss, in this house, yes—Dr. Ivans has entrusted the keys to me until Mr. Robinson shall come tomorrow to take away the furnishings and sell them.

MELIDA

(rising)

Well—when Williams comes tonight, you will give him this letter. You will tell him—no—you will tell him nothing—

(aside)

He will be wretched enough without someone telling him I've suffered. Take this, my friend, take this.

(giving him a half crown, she collapses on a sofa)

PATRICK

Thanks, Miss.

DOCTOR

(coming in behind Melida and resting a hand on her shoulder)

Is it done?

MELIDA

Yes, Father.

DOCTOR

And your poor heart?

MELIDA

God and my love for you will give it strength.

(Émeraude brings in a traveling cape and places in on Melida's shoulders—she hardly notices.)

DOCTOR

Come—let's hurry the trains leaving.

(Melida falls to both knees.)

ÉMERAUDE

Let her say her prayer—it will bring us luck.

MELIDA

(praying)

My God—you who made the world so grand and who are even grander than the world—give me strength—courage—resignation—make our hearts unite under the immensity of heaven which envelops the universe and reunites our souls—if they succumb to pain.

(soft music accompanies Melida's prayer. Rising.)

Here I am, Father. Goodbye, Patrick—don't forget.

PATRICK

Don't worry, Miss.

DOCTOR

Lean on me, poor reed—

(as they leave)

Goodbye to the past—Greetings to the future.

(he leaves last—followed by Melida)

CURTAIN

ACT I

Part of a mining camp. Trees—tents.

A group of three or four miners. On one side are Paul, Catalin, Mobile. On the other, the tent which serves as Mother Joseph's canteen.

MOBILE

Come, Mother Joseph—another plate of your special kangaroo—and a bottle of Brandy.

MOTHER JOSEPH

(coming from the canteen with the two plates requested)

Ah, indeed! The mine has paid today, kids? You dug in the right place?

PAUL

And from what do you conclude that, Mother Joseph?

MOTHER JOSEPH

From the way you treat yourselves.

LE FAUCHEUX

Yes, the expense rejoices you and worries you at the same time. Have no fear—there are nuggets.

MOTHER JOSEPH

Then display them—twenty shillings for the bottle of Brandy, 10 for the spiced kangaroo. Pay up, pay up.

MOBILE

Full of confidence in the customers, Mother Joseph is—bring the scales.

(they weigh the gold—Mother Joseph puts it in a leather sack)

MOTHER JOSEPH

That's fine. Ah, indeed—now who asked for a squirrel in butter?

LE FAUCHEUX

Not me—for fear you'd slip a muskrat in instead—no difficulty, I ate some of your marsupials once—I had a mouth infected for a week, I had trouble eating garlic on garlic—that's not nothing. Is it for you, Marquis?

(to Paul)

PAUL

Excuse me, gentlemen, but I've begged you not to use my title—perhaps one day I'll reclaim it if I make a fortune in the mines—until then my name is Mr. Paul as you are called Mr. Le Faucheux.

MOBILE

Mr. Le Faucheux. Then you call yourself Mr. Le Faucheux?

CATALIN

(to Mother Joseph who remains standing—plate in hand)

Well, let's see—what are you waiting for, Mother? You stare at me—it always seems that I owe you the morsel I put in my mouth—I am uneasy. Who's the sissy that asked for a squirrel?

MOTHER JOSEPH

I'm going to find him.

(She leaves.)

MOBILE

Well it must be that sissy of a Joanne. These Belgian devils—they're accustomed to oysters from Ostend and eggs from Vanneaux.

(to Joanne)

Wasn't it you, Joanne who ordered a squirrel—?

PAUL

Poor boy—if he has some fantasies he can really realize them, for the time he has to live—wait there he is—he can hardly support himself—and he's pale as a corpse.

JOANNE

My friends—somebody come to me and support me—I can't go any further—I'm choking—it seems to me I am going to die.

PAUL

(going to him)

Do me the pleasure of taking my arm, Mr. Joanne.

MOTHER JOSEPH

Can I serve you something, my child?

JOANNE

I have a burning thirst—a glass of fresh water if it is possible.

MOBILE

A carafe of iced water for Mr. Joanne, do you hear, Madam Tortoni.

JOANNE

If you were suffering as I am suffering, Mobile, I wouldn't laugh at you.

MOBILE

Mr. Joanne, we laughed, it's true, but without bad intention it wasn't meant to hurt you, word of honor.

JOANNE

I don't wish you ill for it, Mobile—ah, I'm choking—water for the love of God.

MOBILE

(to Mother Joseph)

Look, didn't you hear him—you stand there like the sign post for your courtier.

CATALIN

(laughing)

He asked for the love of God and Mother Joseph doesn't hear with that ear.

MOTHER JOSEPH

(without releasing the glass)

I put a sugar cube in it. That's a shilling.

CATALIN

What did I tell you!

MOBILE

Meaning you'd let him croak of thirst for want of a shilling—! Here there it is.

JOANNE

(taking the glass, drinking avidly)

Ah—thanks!

MOBILE

It's fatigue which renders you ill, like this—right, my poor Mr. Joanne? You're a son of a family you—that's plain to see—they didn't raise you to wield a pick.

JOANNE

Courage takes the place of habit, the will holds instead of strength. Few people die of pain—it's not that.

CATALIN

What is it then?

JOANNE

Six months ago I received a knife blow which would have done me a great service by killing me right away.

MOBILE

A jealous affair, huh? I bet there's a woman behind it.

JOANNE

No—quite simply a friend who wanted my gold.

LE FAUCHEUX

Give me his description—this friend and if I meet him, I'll bring you back the pieces.

JOANNE

(giving him his hand)

Too late, go.

LE FAUCHEUX

(lowering his pipes)

Who knows—speak anyway.

JOANNE

My father left me a large fortune; in three or four years I saw the end of it—18,000 francs remained to me—my notary in delivering it to me advised me to go to Australia and try my fortune.

PAUL

It was only a question of the miraculous manner by which they enrich themselves at Melbourne or Sidney.

CATALIN

(laughing, pointing to his shoes)

Example: I've been here three years already walking on my boots—which of you is a millionaire? Don't all reply at once.

JOANNE

My 18,000 francs in bank notes were in a little billfold that at night I hid under my pillow.

PAUL

Good precaution—especially if you had a roommate.

JOANNE

I had one of my age almost who'd received a good education—so my distrust appeared to me to be an excess of precaution.

CATALIN

There's never an excess of precaution in these matters.

JOANNE

Still one night, in the midst of my sleep, it seemed to me, as in a dream, that my companion left his bunk and approached mine—soon I thought I felt a hand slide under my bolster—I woke up with a start—but as brief as my passage from slumber to wakefulness had been it was sufficient for my thief to reach the door—I leapt down the stairs and arrived on the bridge at the same time a man who was no other than my roommate. I jumped at his throat yelling "Thief!" but he, seeing himself on the point of being taken with a move as rapid as thought, threw my billfold to the sea—then I rushed to the side where it had fallen—leaning on the handrail to see if it wasn't floating—suddenly, I felt a cold blade of steel penetrate my breast—at the same time, a powerful arm lifted me and hurled me overboard. By luck, a sailor on watch saw what had happened—he threw me a rope that I seized. Max tried to gut him with the same knife he'd struck me with but he was assailed and knocked down by the other sailors before he was able to succeed. They hoisted me on the bridge where I arrived, in a faint.

MOBILE

Eh! I hope he was hanged, this dear Mr. Max.

JOANNE

No.

MOBILE

They were wrong.

CATALIN

Still—he didn't get the reward of martyrdom?

JOANNE

The court in Sidney condemned him to ten years in the galleys.

PAUL

He threw you to the water—an extenuating circumstance.

JOANNE

I arrived here dying, without a sou. For three months I dragged myself about unable to live or die—so much so that without my poor friend Albert, who wished from pity to associate himself with me so as to have the right to give me half his bread, hunger would have finished what the knife was unable to do.

MOBILE

Well, in your place, Mr. Joanne—do you know what I would do?

JOANNE

What would you do?

MOBILE

Have you heard of a brave doctor who lives in Melbourne?

LE FAUCHEUX

Dr. Ivans. As for me, I know him—there's a fine type of man; he picked up a poor miner in the street with his head half crushed. He had him brought to his home, cared for him, cured him, and sent him away with a half crown—

PAUL

There's a doctor who won't make a fortune in Australia.

MOBILE

You must find him.

JOANNE

I'd die before getting halfway there.

MOBILE

Then it will be necessary to send for him, we'll take up a subscription—right, everybody?

PAUL

Mr. Mobile—put me down for 500 pounds sterling.

LE FAUCHEUX

Two hundred for me.

CATALIN

For me—my good will—

JOANNE

Thanks, my friends—thanks. He'll get here to late—I have something that chokes me—I've talked too much; I cannot anymore—oh!

MOTHER JOSEPH

Come rest in my room—

ALL

That's it.

LE FAUCHEUX

There's some good in her—Mother of Grog—

(She leaves with Joanne.)

CATALIN

It hurts me—it makes me thirsty. I ought to take some grog—what do you say to that?

MOBILE

I say one grog; and you, Le Faucheux.

LE FAUCHEUX

As for me, I say three grogs.

PAUL

And for me, I will have some tea.

LE FAUCHEUX

Some tea? Orange pekoe, or English tea, Marquis?

PAUL

Mr. Le Faucheux, I already warned you and your comrades not to call me Marquis—that annoys me and as I am not accustomed to being annoyed, and the first time you do it again, I'll take this revolver here and send you a shot no matter where—you've been warned, right?

LE FAUCHEUX

Yes, Marquis.

PAUL

(drawing his pistol)

ALL

Well, well—don't do anything stupid—for God's sake—look—look—Mr. Paul.

PAUL

I don't make fun of anyone. I don't torment anyone, I don't insult anyone—I don't want anyone to make fun of me, I don't want anyone to torment me, I don't want anyone to insult me! Is that clear?

CATALIN

Anyway, is it insulting you to give you your title?

PAUL

Yes, when I have one red shirt, a straw hat and work trousers— for it means to me that I didn't know how to preserve it properly.

MOTHER JOSEPH

(returning with grog)

Here's the grog you asked for.

CATALIN

Pass me a little tea. I am really ill.

LE FAUCHEUX

(to Mobile)

If you make your fortune what type of sauce will you eat your frogs with?

MOBILE

I've got my plan.

LE FAUCHEUX

And me, too! In a month, the partnership is finished—we will liquidate, I'll make my bow to you and I'm going to Paris—the center of big operations;—there intelligence is sure. The best mines are found between the Madeleine and the Port Saint Martin.

PAUL

It's there they speculate without danger and there you find the true veins which have the best gold—all that's needed is to know how to exploit the confidence and the stupidity of mankind.

LE FAUCHEUX

I shall deploy my spoils and give one and a half percent.

MOBILE

Hurrah! To your health and to your millions.

PAUL

Not bad, Mr. Le Faucheux, not bad—you aren't the inventor but it's well considered.

MOBILE

And you, Catalin, you don't say a thing.

CATALIN

I don't say a thing because your odd jobs aren't worth a sea biscuit.

LE FAUCHEUX

Before criticizing your comrades' plans—expose yours.

MOBILE

Look, Mr. Sailor on vacation, and while waiting for the refitting to catch you—what are you going to do?

CATALIN

I'm arming a warship, a good sailor with a foretop sail, with a top gallant sail and cockatoos. I recruit about 20 ruffians, real dare-devils, and I'll sign myself some letters of mark.

MOBILE

That's fine, you are marked—continue.

CATALIN

I intercept near Port Philippe, the first big clipper that passes; I recognize it as drop sail, I tap it and relieve it of 100 or 500,000 ounces of gold that it has in its hold. After that I sail towards enchanted shores called the Gardens of Armida; we'll put out money for a map of the world and set sail for it. Would you like to be my lieutenant, Mobile?

MOBILE

That suits me, but on condition that once the job is done, we go to Turkey—I'll establish myself as Pasha Mobile, we'll buy houses and odalisques—and we will roll in torrents of voluptuousness. I intend to smoke pipes fifteen feet long and nourish myself only on preserved roses and candies from the harem.

(All the miners drink.)

(singing first verse)

If ever they catch me
wandering through new worlds where fever seizes you,
where the women are withered,
where they don't have any peace,
where you sleep ill, where you don't eat;
I want the devil to take me,
feet in the air—head down.

(refrain)

No, no, no—no more travelin' in this sad distant land.
Let's reach the shore.
Repeating our refrain.
Long live—long live France—
Land of beauty—
Land of hope—
Land of love—

(singing second verse)

Ah, cursed Australia, I bid you adieu—without regret.
Never in life is a more frightful place to be seen—
And full of confidence—
They come here from the ends of Earth.
I shiver to think
My God, my God—
What a descent into Hell.

(refrain)

(repeat)

ALL

To our imminent departure!

MOBILE

To luck.

LE FAUCHEUX

To the ladies, to health, to life.

CATALIN

To all that is beautiful in this world and the other—!

PAUL

To my country—to France!

(Dr. Ivans and Melida enter dressed in riding clothes.)

DOCTOR

(taking off his hat)

To France—the twin sister of England.

ALL

The Doctor.

(they remove their hats)

CATALIN

(running to the tent)

I am going to bring our patient to him.

(going out)

DOCTOR

Pardon, sir—I am indeed at the Ballarat Mine—am I not?

PAUL

(rising and putting on his gloves)

Exactly, sir.

DOCTOR

Do you know a man named Joanne?

PAUL

(pointing to Joanne who enters leaning on Catalin)

There he is.

DOCTOR

In that case, sir—I am going to put myself at your disposal.

MOBILE

(to Joanne)

Then you wrote to him?

JOANNE

No—

DOCTOR

I received a letter requesting my assistance.

(to Melida)

Read it, my child—

MELIDA

(reading)

"Sir, they say you are good and generous! A poor miner friend of mine, who doesn't think he's rich enough to request your help is going to die if you don't come to his aid. I beg you, Doctor, in the name of humanity to make an excursion to the Ballarat Mine and ask for Mr. Joanne. If someday I am lucky, you won't regret inconveniencing yourself on the simple promise of a man who at this moment can only offer you the assurance of his profound gratitude."

JOANNE

Isn't it signed?

MELIDA

Pardon, sir—it is signed: heart of gold—and that sufficed for my father.

MOBILE

(to Paul)

It's really fine what you did there, Mr. Paul.

PAUL

Me.

MOBILE

Yes, you—only a Marquis is capable of writing such a letter—to us; perhaps the idea might come—but the writing—

(to Doctor)

It was useless for you to hide your name, as for me I recognize the signature—Marquis one day we will both be drunk. I will ask permission to embrace you.

PAUL

My friend, you are giving me one of those lessons which are profitable if God extends life to those who receive it. That letter is not from me, Miss, and I regret that sincerely.

DOCTOR

What is the nature of the wound received, sir?

JOANNE

A knife blow in the right side of the chest; I suffer at the least movement I make.

DOCTOR

Can you stand?

JOANNE

Yes, with help—doctor?

MOBILE and PAUL

(rushing to him)

What do you think!

DOCTOR

Look—stand straight

(listening with his ear against the breast)

The Devil! A lesion between the pleura and the lung. They did well to write me, sir.

LE FAUCHEUX

(uneasily)

But it's not too late is it?

DOCTOR

No but—

(to Joanne)

It was in the nick of time. Do you have some courage, sir?

JOANNE

I have some.

DOCTOR

Your wound necessitates a painful operation but which, performed by an experienced hand, involves no danger. Is there a room to be found here?

MOTHER JOSEPH

You come rest in my room.

DOCTOR

After the operation is performed, in a week it will no longer appear.

JOANNE

(smiling)

If more than a week is required doctor, don't trouble yourself about it.

DOCTOR

Lean on my arm.

JOANNE

Breathing is difficult—that's what makes me suffer the most.

DOCTOR

Well, in a week, I don't go back on my word, you'll be able to run for the prize in a race.

(They go into the tent.)

MOTHER JOSEPH

Remain here, Miss. I am going to be back right away.

MELIDA

Poor young man—he seems very interesting.

ALBERT

(in the wings)

Joanne! Joanne!

(rushing in)

Where is he?

MELIDA

Mr. Joanne? He is in there with my father, the Doctor.

ALBERT

The Doctor! He received my letter—he's come—ah! What luck! Am I such a child? Would you believe, Miss—I'm in greater fear than Joanne. At the thought of this injury, they're going to do him—the sweat runs down my face and I tremble like a leaf agitated by the wind. What do you expect! Nature made a mistake. It gave me the features of a man and the heart of a woman. When I was a child and my mother pricked her finger with her needle, I wept for the whole day—for having seen her lose a drop of blood.

MELIDA

(trying to distract him)

Do you still have your mother?

ALBERT

In Europe! That's called having one's mother! Yes, since she lives, yes, living until this moment, I hope to see her again. We were really poor, and I said to myself in parting—Bah! Some months are soon passed! I didn't count on the weakness of my heart—the months have become centuries.

MELIDA

Have you been in the mines a long while?

ALBERT

Since—an eternity by my count—a year—by the reckoning of the calendar. Ah, now that I am rich, I will give half of my blood to shorten the distance that separates me from London—it's so far.

MELIDA

Alas—!

ALBERT

But pardon, Miss—I am speaking to you of my fears and my hopes as if they could be of interest to you.

MELIDA

Aren't we compatriots, sir? And at 5,000 leagues from our native land, aren't we more than compatriots—aren't we brothers?

(a moaning)

ALBERT

(shaking)

Ah, Miss! Didn't you hear a moaning?

MELIDA

No—it's the wind.

ALBERT

Poor Joanne! If you knew what an admirable nature! I really want to see England again—right? I can leave the mines when I choose—since I am rich now—eh—well, I won't leave until Joanne's cured—then I will take a passage on best sailing ship—

MELIDA

I hope that the boat which takes you back to your mother has the wings of a bird, sir.

ALBERT

If you ask God in your prayers, it will go more swiftly than a humming bird.

(another moan)

Oh—that time I really heard it—egoist that I am, I was only thinking of myself.

(enter Mother Joseph)

MOTHER JOSEPH

There, there then! It's all over—the Doctor is a fine man! And a pleasure to see him at work! Only he was paler than the patient himself.

(Max and Cooper enter but without being seen.)

MELIDA

Would you see, Madam, if our horses have eaten the hay, and give the order if they've been unsaddled—that they be readied.

MOTHER JOSEPH

But you cannot be thinking of leaving this evening I hope?

MELIDA

That's my father's intention Madam.

MOTHER JOSEPH

Impossible—the roads are not safe during the day, but at night there are real cut throats.

MELIDA

What to do?

MOTHER JOSEPH

Spend the night here. Your father ought not to be really difficult—he'll be satisfied with a bench—as for you—you will share my room.

COOPER

I would offer her half of mine as well.

MAX

Shut up.

MELIDA

If my father decides to stay I will accept your offer with gratitude—for I feel I am fatigued; it was farther from here to Melbourne than they told us.

MOTHER JOSEPH

Nearly twenty miles—and by such roads as should be counted double.

MELIDA

What a savage looking place! Everywhere the verdure of the trees is gay—here it's of a mortal sadness.

(noticing Max in the shadows)

My God!

MOTHER JOSEPH

What's the matter with you?

MELIDA

It seemed to me—that there in the shadows I saw a man who was spying on us—wait, wait, there in the distance—there are two now—and they seem to slink away.

MOTHER JOSEPH

Miners or pickpockets. Bah! No need to be preoccupied with so few—there are lots of them.

MELIDA

How sad the trees are! As if this vegetation were languishing—!

MOTHER JOSEPH

Ah! It won't languish very long—the January sun will devour it in a week.

MELIDA

Decidedly a country that grows flowers is better than one that breeds gold.

(goes in sighing)

MOTHER JOSEPH

Happily, not everyone is of her opinion.

(Max and Cooper appear again farther off.)

MAX

An adorable person, white like snow, graceful as a bird—! Oh—it's plain she comes to us from the other side of the Atlantic.

COOPER

Yes, but this one, my dear fellow, is forbidden fruit.

MAX

Why's that?

COOPER

Because—the daughter of a doctor—you must marry her.

MAX

Well—we'll marry her. I have no aversion to marriage.

COOPER

Yes, but to marry one must have papers in order and I think on that chapter, yours leave something to be desired.

MAX

If that young girl were to be the daughter of the governor of Melbourne—from the moment Max says—she belongs to me.

COOPER

Well—?

MAX

Well—she'll belong to Max!

COOPER

I'm not curious but I'd like to see that.

MAX

We'll talk about it again. The pressing thing is to busy ourselves with that ninny who came to tell us he had more gold than he could carry—as if to tempt us.

COOPER

(aside)

There's yet another unpleasant job—go—little worm! Is it really necessary to speak of his affairs to the whole world?

MAX

As for me, my opinion is that it's necessary to begin with Joanne.

COOPER

Joanne is a man three-quarters dead; the other quarter is the Doctor's concern. Let's let him alone.

MAX

I'm going to join the little fellow. Be alert, I will give you my orders in an hour.

(Exit Max.)

COOPER

(along, watching him leave)

I will give you my orders. Is he sure of himself—I'm not yet his servant. And when I think that in all friendships there is always an oppressor and an oppressed—it's stronger than I am! He insults me, and I say—keep at it—he beats me and I say—do more—his look fascinates me—his voice bewitches me—his will dominates me; he tells me go—and I march—despite myself—it's like magic, it's not explainable. Fine—here come the others.

(he hides)

ALBERT

(returning, leaning on Max)

Everybody's drunk. I got everybody to drink to Joanne's recovery—to the health of the doctor, to his charming daughter, to mine—and we drank so much, drank so much—so much—that it makes me weak in the legs—

(unsteady on my feet)

—got to give them their head—

MAX

Lean on my arm. I'm going to accompany you.

ALBERT

(stopping)

But since I tell you, my friend—my good friend—my dear friend—I don't want to return to my hovel—come then, the Earth is good for foxes and badgers—I'm going to wait here until my friend Joanne's cured. It won't be long—the Doctor said—everything went fine.

MAX

Yes, but he recommended that no one go into the room here until tomorrow morning—what will you do here until tomorrow morning?

ALBERT

Me—I'll play cards. I'll drink punch—I'll smoke 3 shilling cigars—I am rich—my money belts full of gold.

MAX

My dear sir—you are committing a great imprudence in shouting this to the rooftops.

ALBERT

To the rooftops—and where do you see any rooftops?

MAX

You say, then, that your gold—ah—you want to see my claim—well—well—it's there, behind that rock—I am going to show it to you.

COOPER

(aside)

Oh—the larks, the larks—

(aloud)

Should I keep an eye out?

MAX

Follow, imbecile.

COOPER

Thanks, Mr. Max.

ALBERT

Heavens—your name is Max?

MAX

No—Robert.

ALBERT

Ah, I thought I heard "Max." You see I don't like that name. It's the name of a man who tried to murder Joanne. Do you know him—Joanne? He's my friend—you, too—he's my friend—you, too—the beer you made me drink is good—only it smells more like Brandy than bourbon—

MAX

You were saying that the claim where you found your gold—?

ALBERT

It's true—you see—the vein goes—like this side of Europe—and soon—I will go—by way of the vein—

(they go to the wings)

I'm lying down—go to sleep.

(utters a terrific scream)

Ah!

(a second weaker scream)

Ah!

MOBILE

(running in with miners)

Did you hear a moan?

CATALIN

Yes.

MOBILE

Did you hear, Mr. Paul?

PAUL

(standing)

Yes.

MOBILE

A man's escaping.

(he rushes)

After the thief! After the murderer!

(Paul fires a shot. They run in all directions)

MINERS

They're bringing somebody! This way, this way.

DOCTOR

What's wrong?

VOICES

A crime.

MOBILE

(looking at the body)

Albert! It's Albert!

MOBILE

So young—so full of hopes—!

PAUL

Wounded or dead?

DOCTOR

Wait—

JOANNE

(appearing)

Albert—! Wounded! Dead perhaps—my friend, my poor friend.

ALBERT

Joanne! The scoundrel's killed me—he's the same one—

JOANNE

The same! Who's that? Look, answer me—

ALBERT

Max—he shivered when I said your name—then—there's only one man who in the world who hides cruelty behind an eternal smile—you described him to me—I should have recognized him—but I only saw my happiness.

JOANNE

Oh—Doctor in the name of heaven—save him.

ALBERT

(rising)

I wanted to live so much. Joanne you will return to London, you will see my mother, poor mother—she had my first smiles, my first kiss—well, you will tell her that I send her my last tear—my last thought, my last sigh.

DOCTOR

Dead!

JOANNE

I will avenge him!

ALL THE MINERS

Yes, yes—we will avenge him.

CURTAIN

ACT II

The interior of the Doctor's dwelling.

LOUISA

(dusting)

This hellish country—the dust doesn't give us a moment's rest.

(The noise of cannon can be heard.)

LOUISA

That announces the arrival of the steamboat. We are going to have news of Mr. Williams.

ÉMERAUDE

May God will it, for my poor Melida no longer sleeps—what were you telling me yesterday, Louisa?

LOUISA

On what subject, Miss?

ÉMERAUDE

About this American, our cousin—with whom your friend, the Parisian, is living?

LOUISA

The Parisian is working there because you could no longer keep him. I was telling you that this American must be very rich—to judge by appearances, at least.

ÉMERAUDE

Louisa, the Parisian must perform a service for me, still.

LOUISA

Ah! He will do it with great pleasure.

ÉMERAUDE

A rich and showy man like his new master must love beautiful jewels.

(turning her head and giving her a ring)

Here!

LOUISA

You want to part with this ring?

ÉMERAUDE

Alas! It's necessary. Poor ring! My father gave it to my mother to celebrate my arrival in this world—and my poor mother gave me the name of this stone to be the treasure of her memories.

LOUISA

And you are going to sell it?

ÉMERAUDE

We are without money—my father doesn't know how to deal with misfortunes—he mustn't know of it.

LOUISA

Don't worry, Miss.

PARISIAN

(in the wings)

Why it's a scandal—such things have never been seen—why I'm going to shout thief in the middle of the street.

LOUISA

There—Miss—that's the Parisian now—

LOUISA

But who've you got it in for, my poor Parisian?

PARISIAN

Excuse me, Miss—but it's because I am furious—can you believe that I returned from market with eggs big as partridge eggs—a shilling a piece—why you must be rich like Mr. Fulton to be able to get them and eat omelets.

LOUISA

Then your master is very rich?

PARISIAN

Like the late Croesus! But I won't be less ashamed when I present him my accounts—dinners at fifty pounds without counting the wine—125 French francs for a single meal!

ÉMERAUDE

If he receives a lot of company.

PARISIAN

Why, not a cat! He always eats alone—three pounds for lunch—five pounds for dinner—then the teas, the sugar, the fruits—that amounts to 300 francs a day—the one without the other—I don't know how he keeps it up, word of honor.

LOUISA

And he never makes observations?

PARISIAN

No indeed! He pays to the last farthing. That's what enrages me—if he made remarks—I would tell him—come to the market with me—come on and you will see—

ÉMERAUDE

Always gay—always happy—that's true riches.

PARISIAN

But, pardon—I didn't come to tell you all this—I came to tell you—

LOUISA

He doesn't know anything.

PARISIAN

It's indignation that carries me away. I came to tell you—on the part of Mr. Fulton, that he knows that the young ladies love flowers a lot, and that as he has the most beautiful in Melbourne in his garden—he invites you to come pick them as much as you like.

LOUISA

But how does Mr. Fulton expect these young ladies to go to the home of a bachelor?

PARISIAN

Why that's not an obstacle. Mr. Fulton has some claims that he must exploit at the mines so that he's always on the move. So when Mr. Fulton's not there—like today for example—these ladies will come and no one will have anything to say.

ÉMERAUDE

If he had been presented to us, but when one has never seen people—

PARISIAN

He knows you. Miss Melida, especially—he opened his eyes when he spoke of it.

ÉMERAUDE

Ah! Where did he meet her?

PARISIAN

I don't know anything about it—but if I hadn't told him she was engaged, I believe he would have asked for her in marriage—he dreams about her when sleeping.

ÉMERAUDE

(aside)

That's strange.

(to Louisa)

Give me the ring. I will go to a jeweler.

LOUISA

Are you coming, Parisian?

PARISIAN

Don't come close—the sun has made my butter melt.

(leaving)

MELIDA

(to Émeraude)

(entering)

Ah, sister—what a joy that one doesn't die of joy.

ÉMERAUDE

(going to her)

You've received news of Williams, right?

MELIDA

It's not only that, today the steamship arrived. At the first shot of the cannon, father and I rushed to the balcony, holding hands—well—from our observatory we saw a man running like a fool on the road from Melbourne.

ÉMERAUDE

It was Williams?

MELIDA

I was dazzled. My eyes were shut; father went out to meet him and I've only had the strength to come throw myself in your arms.

ÉMERAUDE

(hugging her)

Poor friend! Suppose you were mistaken?

MELIDA

Oh—no—go—feel my heart.

(taking her hand)

WILLIAMS

(entering)

Melida.

(Melida lets out a scream and collapses in his arms.)

ÉMERAUDE

It's really him.

(The Doctor enters.)

WILLIAMS

Yes, Melida—it's me, it's really me! Ah, indeed—were you no longer expecting me?

MELIDA

Oh! Yes—right, Father?

ÉMERAUDE

We were expecting you every day, sir, every hour, every minute—now you are here, our poor hearts are going to have a little rest.

WILLIAMS

Darling sisters.

DOCTOR

(to Melida)

Well—didn't I tell you—one only separates hearts that want to be separated

MELIDA

I'm so happy that I'm afraid I'm dreaming.

WILLIAMS

Four months of waiting and five months at sea. A dull calm, not a breath of wind not an hour of breeze—you would have said that the elements had lost their breath. I strode the bridge of the ship imagining, doubtless that this hurried step was going to push it forward. I thought that I would go mad! The captain wanted to toss me into the sea; he said I brought bad luck. Ah, if you knew what I suffered there in London. At 10 o'clock, I arrived at the rendezvous you had given me—my heart was full of joy; I was going to leave with you; everything would be shared between us—we ought to have only one future. I recall that terrible moment as if I were still there. I entered—not a sound, not a whisper—the clock itself seemed to have stopped at the moment you left, Melida. Melida, I said, all joyous as I was—to inform you I had obtained a loan of 4,000 pounds sterling. Patrick was alone—he gave me this letter in which you said to me, "I will die if I never see you again." Oh—then I shouted—"If I have to cross the ocean in a canoe you will see me dearly beloved of my heart." Here I am, Melida.

MELIDA

Dear Williams.

WILLIAMS

Well, now—let's see—where are we, dear Doctor? And all our grand hopes?

DOCTOR

Ah, my poor friend! Dreams! It's no longer a profession—it's a job—I'm no longer a doctor—I'm a veterinarian. All the same, one could make one's fortune here by demanding to be paid in advance—but how to see the poor suffer without trying to help them. It's true, I forget my troubles a bit by consoling those who are more wretched than I. But you see, dear Williams, what is most clear in all this is that I don't have the heart needed in this cursed country.

MELIDA

Trust in God, father!

DOCTOR

Do you hear them? Everything is still fine with them.

WILLIAMS

Yes, everything is fine, since I am here. First of all, I don't know where you are regarding money, but they're still 250 pounds sterling in this purse—which are yours—since they are mine.

DOCTOR

Williams!

WILLIAMS

Keep them, I don't need them. A friend, who still had too much for himself, loaned them to me at the time of my departure.

DOCTOR

But that was to do business—a speculation of some sort.

WILLIAMS

First of all, I detest business and speculation. But wait! God is taking a hand in my affairs—

MELIDA

Can you imagine father? But is there only enough for him?

WILLIAMS

There's enough for everybody, don't worry. Can you believe that my good star caused me to find the new governor of Melbourne on the same ship as myself?

DOCTOR

Has he fallen ill—and is he a new patient you are bringing me?

WILLIAMS

He's in marvelous shape—and may God protect his health—what was I telling you—I don't know any more.

MELIDA

You were on the same steamship as the governor.

WILLIAMS

Yes—and this is what he told me as we set foot on land "Run, kiss your fiancée, my dear Williams and come back right away to see me—I'm going to make them present me with the accounts—and if there's a vacancy which suits you—it's yours."

MELIDA

Ah! The excellent man!

WILLIAMS

So that, you see, I ran, I kissed you—you are going to let me tell you again and again that I love you, Melida—with all my heart—with all my soul—like a madman—then take to my heels—and run back to the governor.

MELIDA

Are you going to leave me?

WILLIAMS

Oh—this time, don't worry, Melida—it won't be for a long while—but I mustn't allow enough time for his good will to cool. Plague! If my place were to be taken—!

MELIDA

Which one?

WILLIAMS

Which one—I don't know.

DOCTOR

(looking at Melida)

At last, I will only see smiles. It's about time—go, Melida, you're weeping—Émeraude's weeping to see her cry—I was really ready to give up my lost illusions—once the trio begins, I don't know on what note it will stop.

(laughing)

(Williams shakes his hand. Shouts outside, "Help! Help!")

DOCTOR

What is it this time?

(Doctor and Émeraude run to the window.)

MELIDA

How happy I am!

WILLIAMS

Not more than I.

DOCTOR

Doubtless a horse has just thrown its rider.

ÉMERAUDE

They are saying it's the horse of our neighbor, Mr. Fulton.

WILLIAMS

(laughing)

Ah—we have a neighbor?

MELIDA

(laughing, taking his arm)

We have more than one, sir.

ÉMERAUDE

Father, are Melida and I permitted to escort Mr. Williams for the first mile?

DOCTOR

Yes, only don't get lost on the way.

MELIDA

Oh—don't worry, Father.

DOCTOR

Shall we expect you for dinner?

WILLIAMS

I don't know—but what I know is I will be here as soon as I can.

LOUISA

(entering as the two girls are about to leave with Williams)

Doctor! Doctor! Good heaven, Mr. Williams! Ah—now that's lucky—Oh, my God! My God—what a misfortune!

DOCTOR

Good luck—misfortune, explain yourself.

LOUISA

Fright, surprise—I no longer know where I am.

WILLIAMS

(to Émeraude)

Your arm, dear Melida, goodbye—Doctor.

DOCTOR

Good luck, my boy—

(they leave)

(to Louisa)

Look, explain yourself if you can.

LOUISA

Ah—! It's coming back to me—you saw a horse run away, right?

DOCTOR

Yes, it passed between our windows.

LOUISA

Well, it was Mr. Fulton's. It seems it was so frightened in the woods where he shied and threw Mr. Fulton ten feet—head against a tree.

DOCTOR

And he was killed.

LOUISA

No—but he's not doing well.

DOCTOR

I'm going there.

LOUISA

No—it's not worth the trouble, Parisian, give the order to bring him here.

PARISIAN

Come in! Come in!

LOUISA

The Doctor is here.

(opens door)

DOCTOR

This way, this way—there—on the sofa he will be fine—place him gently.

(taking his pulse)

This man must be bled right away—he has congestion.

(The Parisian enters, followed by Fulton on stretcher. He's half hidden by those carrying him. The doctor bleeds the patient, but the audience cannot see this.)

LOUISA

(pulling the Parisian downstage)

What an event? But how did it happen?

PARISIAN

(to Louisa)

No one knows—at least not very much—they saw Mr. Fulton go on horseback into the little woods a mile from here—then they heard two or three pistol shots, then they saw the horse come out of the woods covered with foam and blood.

LOUISA

The blood of his master, doubtless.

PARISIAN

His own, poor beast—he took a shot in the chest.

LOUISA

Poor young man! He must have been attacked by bandits.

(The Doctor takes Fulton, who has fainted and places him on the couch with his head facing the garden.)

DOCTOR

There—that's taken care of. Now my friends—leave us alone, Parisian and me. We need peace and quiet. Go.

(The stretcher carriers leave.)

PARISIAN

Tell me, Doctor—would you say things are improving?

DOCTOR

He's got a burning fever.

PARISIAN

That's well done—he never wanted to listen to me. Oh, if I'd been his master rather than his servant.

(Fulton seems to open his eyes)

Mr. Fulton—do you recognize me? It's me, Mr. Fulton—and that's Dr. Ivans.

FULTON

(delirious)

Don't come near me—don't come any closer—! The first one to touch me is a dead man.

PARISIAN

(aside)

He takes us for robbers.

FULTON

(laughing)

You want to arrest me to get the reward?

(starting up)

Touch me if you dare!

PARISIAN

Right! Now he takes us for policemen.

FULTON

(advancing on the Parisian who he grabs by the throat)

You want to grab me, take me to prison—you think I'm without strength—I'm going to strangle you.

PARISIAN

Why he squeezes in earnest—but I am very strong, too—

(takes him by the arm and places him on the sofa)

DOCTOR

You see plainly, the man is delirious.

PARISIAN

So be it—but that's no reason to strangle me.

FULTON

(beaten)

Mercy! Don't denounce me—I have gold—lots of gold. I'll give it to you.

DOCTOR

(to himself)

Yet another conscience struggling in a broken body.

(to Parisian)

Is he subject to these fits?

PARISIAN

Yes, sometimes at night, I heard something like terrible disputes in his room—but one cannot go in—he barricades himself every night—he says that he dreams out loud.

FULTON

(still delirious)

That man lied—what do you mean that he recognized me? The

night was black—the moon was hidden behind a cloud—blood? You see quite well the blood is mine.

(he rises—takes a few steps, then staggers and falls into the arms of the Doctor who places him back on the canopy)

DOCTOR

(to Parisian)

Run to your master, get another set of clothes so that when he feels better he'll be able to go. I will take care of him meantime—go.

PARISIAN

But if he fell on you.

(the Doctor makes him sit)

(Parisian leaves by the back)

DOCTOR

This man's delirium resembles a real terror. Miserable country where one never knows to whom one speaks.

FULTON

(coming to himself and looking at the Doctor with terror)

Where am I? What has happened to me?

DOCTOR

You're at Dr. Ivans—you took a fall from your horse—they

brought you here unconscious—I bled you and coming to yourself, you've been delirious.

FULTON

(uneasy and concerned, rises and supports himself on the back of the sofa)

And in my delirium I spoke, right? According to my custom, I took trees for giants, all men for evildoers?

DOCTOR

You were delirious.

FULTON

Ah—what did I say to you?

DOCTOR

Taking your servant for a policeman, you beat him.

FULTON

Poor lad—his fortune is made.

DOCTOR

(aside)

No need to tell him that Parisian gave him back in kind.

FULTON

(to himself)

Oh—wretched nature which cannot command its conscience!

(aloud)

Wait, dear doctor, I have to confide in you.

(sitting down)

For perhaps my words gave you a bad opinion of me. Isn't a doctor a confessor?

(the doctor takes a chair and draws it close to Fulton)

DOCTOR

It's really difficult when ministering to the wounds of the body, not to minister to those of the soul at the same time.

FULTON

(smiling)

Since my good fortune has brought me into your house I wish to be able to return. I am better; I owe you my life.

DOCTOR

(always with suspicion)

Oh—you exaggerate, sir!

FULTON

Allow me to think so.

(the doctor sits down)

I was born in America. An irresistible vocation led me toward the sea. I shipped aboard the Washington, during a voyage which took us to Batavia; the captain took a strong dislike to me—he was a brutal man and action rapidly followed threats. I more than once controlled my rage, but one day, carried away by the violence of my character, I went for his throat, I forced him to the ground and held him under my knee until he asked for mercy—an hour later, I was in irons. By luck in the roadstead, my shipmates revolted and set me free. I profited by fleeing and sought refuge in Batavia, at the home of a worthy Dutchman, who hid me so well that I escaped all searches—but I almost went mad! The result is that at night, sometimes, I wake with a start—believing myself pursued, taken, arrested.

DOCTOR

Yes, yes, I understand everything. You put yourself on the defensive.

(aside)

The poor Parisian knows something of that.

FULTON

Finally, I came to Australia, living like a savage. I went to the mines where I found an inexhaustible vein of gold. After having exploited it myself, I had it exploited by men in my pay and now I am rich. Ah, Doctor, how happy I would be without this condemnation which weighs on me. I am a deserter accused of having willfully murdered my captain—perhaps one day I'll get the judgment annulled—but for that, it takes time.

DOCTOR

(rising)

I would never have asked you for your secret, sir, but I am happy you confided it in me.

(moves his chair to the left)

FULTON

(shaking)

Someone!

(aside)

It's she! Oh—now I'm part of the house.

(rises)

MELIDA

(enters—noticing Fulton)

Ah, excuse me, father—we didn't know—

(makes a movement to leave)

(Émeraude enters.)

FULTON

Doctor, do me the honor of presenting me.

DOCTOR

(passing in front of his daughter)

Sir, my two daughters, Émeraude and Melida—

(they are silent)

Children—Mr. Fulton, our neighbor to whom I just rendered a little service.

FULTON

The least thing, ladies; the Doctor saved my life.

DOCTOR

There you go again.

FULTON

The Doctor's right—for he's done more—he has just authorized me to come present him my thanks and consequently to offer you my homage—

ÉMERAUDE

That will be a great honor for us, sir.

MELIDA

(low)

What are you saying?

ÉMERAUDE

(low)

I'm replying politely to a compliment.

FULTON

They told me you love flowers, ladies, and I ordered my servant to put my garden in its entirety at your disposal.

MELIDA

We won't abuse it, sir.

FULTON

And you will be wrong! You see, I give you the example of indiscretion by remaining in your home, but excuse me, I am still very weak.

(falls to couch)

The Doctor can bear witness.

DOCTOR

Yes—the gentleman will remain here until tomorrow.

FULTON

But this room is without doubt yours.

DOCTOR

(passing behind the couch)

No—it's detached completely from the rest of the apartment. It's a place where I perform operations. It's far enough off, so that my daughters can't hear the groans of the patients.

WILLIAMS

(entering)

Well, dear father—when I told you that my friend, the governor—

(noticing Fulton)

Ah, pardon, sir.

DOCTOR

(to Williams)

Mr. Fulton.

WILLIAMS

Excuse me, sir—but joy blinded my eyes—I thought I was with family.

DOCTOR

(presenting Williams)

Mr. Williams Nelson, my friend, soon to be my son-in-law, for he's to marry my dear Melida.

(shaking Williams' hand)

FULTON

(aside)

Her fiancé—perhaps her husband—but not yet.

(aloud)

I will take my share, sir, of all happy news that you bring home to the Doctor.

DOCTOR

Speak.

FULTON

I beg you—

WILLIAMS

Well, father, I was telling you that the governor kept his promise, everything is signed. It's a great favor to obtain one of these places—there are a hundred applicants for one chosen. Judge then, a place paying 1,000 pounds sterling.

MELIDA

A thousand pounds sterling.

FULTON

May I ask you what place you are going to occupy, sir?

WILLIAMS

I am nominated escort officer who escorts the gold from the mines at Ballarat to Melbourne.

FULTON

(startled)

A great place, indeed, sir—

(smiling)

But dangerous—

WILLIAMS

The Gold Thieves from what they say are rough adversaries, but they'll learn who they're dealing with—forbidden to take prisoners—order to kill them without mercy—and in my opinion, very just.

FULTON

(rising)

My compliments, sir! You will often be escorting gold belonging to me. Defend it carefully.

WILLIAMS

(sizing him up in his turn)

Count on me.

DOCTOR

(taking Fulton's hand)

Come, come—let's leave my patient in peace. There—the fever is returning.

FULTON

Me! No, Doctor. I swear to you.

DOCTOR

(looking at him)

Your eyes are shining—your hand is burning—come—calm down—especially some rest.

(Everyone leaves. The Doctor shakes Williams' hand—who leaves by the back—then he leaves with his daughters by the left.)

WILLIAMS

Later, father, later—

FULTON

(watches them go off—then when they are gone, his face changes its expression. He rises, walks around stealthily and finally leans on the chimney)

Calm when I am experiencing the most violent emotion of my life. This woman for whom I would give all the stars in the firmament and all the gold of the Earth has just thrown herself before me, into the arms of another; ah, the Doctor is right—I have fever—

(looks at himself in the mirror)

And with that, pale as a dead man—without strength. I'm having visions. It seemed to me—I saw Mr. Cooper in the forest where I attacked the miners that I thought were defenseless—I was mistaken; if I could leave—! I can hardly sustain myself—oh—Williams—the idea of his luck is driving me mad.

(walks across the stage and collapses in the sofa on the right)

PARISIAN

(enters with a dressing gown)

It's me, sir—perhaps one can enter without exposing oneself to blows. Here's clothing.

FULTON

(smiling)

Poltroon—who asked for this?

(rising)

PARISIAN

(helping him dress)

The Doctor. It seems you are better. I congratulate myself—ah, I found a funny chap at the door. He wanted to enter by force to speak to you.

FULTON

Here?

PARISIAN

He's said that you had lost a wallet.

FULTON

Yes, with some banknotes in it—a considerable enough amount even.

PARISIAN

Well, the man found it and is there—he's got a singular aspect. If he doesn't relate to you, I think he's come to—

FULTON

—to give me a billfold containing 1,000 pounds sterling; in any country in the world, that's good—but in Australia—that's magnificent. Let him in and leave me—

PARISIAN

Come in, the gentleman agrees to receive you—as for me, I wouldn't do it—still.

(he leaves.)

(Enter Cooper disguised, so Fulton doesn't at first recognize him. He goes to Fulton.)

COOPER

Here my good, sir—here's your billfold.

FULTON

Thanks, my friend—but wait.

(looks in the wallet to give him a reward)

Well!

COOPER

What are you looking for?

FULTON

I'm looking—I'm looking for the 1,000 pounds that were in this billfold!

COOPER

Useless!

FULTON

What do you mean, useless!

COOPER

They're no longer there.

FULTON

And where are they?

COOPER

(rising and going to him)

In my pocket.

FULTON

In your pocket?

COOPER

Eh, yes, friend, Max—not counting that you owe me four times that at least.

FULTON

Cooper?

COOPER

Ah, it's really nice that the gentleman deigns to recognize his old friends.

FULTON

(looking everywhere)

Look! What do you want from me?

COOPER

Oh—he's charming—what do I want from him—? He asks that, that dear Max.

FULTON

Shut up! Shut up!

COOPER

That's easy to say—shut up—shut up—but as for me, my heart is full of reproaches—and I don't want to shut up.

FULTON

You will make them to me much later—in my home—but not here.

COOPER

(rising)

In your home! You have a home?—You?

FULTON

Yes.

COOPER

You are really lucky. It's true with my share of the loot—you could have a home, a nice one—and where is your home?

FULTON

Here's my card.

COOPER

He has cards—excuse me—Fulton—ah, your name is Fulton now—? Let's see the address. Oh, I can't read writing as fine as this—you'll escort me there—I won't leave you.

FULTON

But shut up—do you want to ruin me?

COOPER

Oh! No—I am too happy to have found you again—you really gave me the slip, ingrate.

FULTON

Silence!

COOPER

Ah, you put on grand airs—? Well, I won't shut up—we are not in your home here—you're going to listen to me.

FULTON

(uneasy, looking everywhere)

You're going to listen to me.

COOPER

No use having nerves—I won't shorten things by a syllable. Let's recapitulate.

FULTON

Will you ever finish?

COOPER

(sitting)

I am going to begin—and if eloquence carries me away—

FULTON

I will go mad with rage.

COOPER

You've already duped me several times! You're more tricky than I am.

FULTON

I will give you all that you want but leave.

COOPER

Yah, yah, yah—I no longer fall for that. You are playing the gentleman at the expense of your friend.

FULTON

What torture!

COOPER

You didn't always say that when we were there chained together in the prison at Sydney. You, for having thrown Joanne into the sea, me, for having killed a man who struck the woman I love right in front of me because that woman didn't love him any more. I only loved once—without that misfortune I would never have known scum like you.

FULTON

(furious)

Cooper!

COOPER

(calmly)

Take care—they're going to hear you—you called me your friend, your savior, because it was thanks to my escape plan that instead of doing ten years, you did ten days.

FULTON

I was going to find you, for I have a big deal to propose to you.

(more and more uneasily)

Give me a meeting in the forest.

COOPER

Have you seen the moon, my boy, have you seen the moon? That's where I am going to give you a rendezvous. I'd have time to take a seed and grow it in the woods while waiting for you. A good business—I'll be with it—after we've liquidated the first. Meanwhile, I'm not leaving you.

FULTON

(terrified)

They're coming! Not a word or we are lost! Shut up, Cooper and I will make you earn tons of gold.

COOPER

Is he sweet to me!

FULTON

You won't leave me; but we cannot leave here together.

COOPER

(aside)

Ah—now we're there! There must be several exits here.

(aloud)

Don't think of it, my little Max! Leave you for a minute in the condition you are in! Let's go—before being your creditor, I am your friend.

FULTON

(sighing)

Let's go since you desire it.

COOPER

I'm doing better than that; I wish it.

FULTON

(to Parisian who enters)

You will deliver this on my behalf to the doctor.

PARISIAN

Do you need him?

FULTON

No, no! I don't wish to disturb him, on the contrary this brave man has just brought me news which obliges me to return home instantly—here—

(gives him a bag of gold)

I repeat to you—you will take this on my part to Dr. Ivans.

(with dignity—to Cooper)

Come, brave man.

COOPER

How he said that: Come—brave man—how not to adore this creature! Would you do me the honor of leaning on my arm, Mr. Fulton?

FULTON

No—thanks.

COOPER

I follow at Milord's side.

PARISIAN

(alone—watching them leave)

Is there any common sense, I ask you—in leaving with a man who looks like that? He's going to get his head broken for sure. Ah, my word, he can say what he likes—I won't lose sight of him.

CURTAIN

ACT III

The forest.

Jason and Jenny is seated on the trunk of a tree eating an apple.

JENNY

God, oh, God! How ugly the native plants of this country are.

JASON

They are even more stupid then they are ugly—let's get going.

JENNY

I'm hungry.

JASON

You can eat on the way.

JENNY

I'm tired.

JASON

You'll rest as you walk.

JENNY

You won't trick me again so soon—and that doesn't rest me at all.

JASON

Let's reach town before dark—they say thieves hide in the trees—perhaps you're seated on a robber chief.

JENNY

(rising and looking at the tree trunk)

Poltroon—go!

JASON

Poltroon—no. Prudent, yes. It's been 10 months we were working in the mines to earn enough to allow us to return to Ireland—and I don't want to risk—.

JENNY

Your life—and me—who got married to have a protector—a prop, a support.

JASON

Look, little wife—how do you expect me to support you if I let myself be killed?

JENNY

(preparing to leave)

He's always right! This is a trip which I'll remember—me—who counted on finding a fortune here.

JASON

It is here—only it's not visible to everybody—and it has its caprices. Anyway, I don't complain since I met you. I left alone—I'll return with two—maybe three—

(Fulton appears in the back in the costume of a hunter)

JENNY

You emigrated because you wouldn't support yourself—what are you going to do with us?

JASON

(taking her in his arms)

Love—gives courage—I'm going to work like four—you don't know what may happen. Come on—

JENNY

Let's go—we are rich in love—that treasure is worth more than any other—when one knows how to manage it.

JASON

It's worth more than any other.

(They go out.)

FULTON

(watching them)

I thought they would never go—to love! to be loved by the woman one loves—oh, yes—that ought to be the greatest happiness. I am jealous of birds who make their nests in the branches. Melida—Melida—I need all your smiles or all your tears. Let's orient ourselves—let's see—Indeed, it's here that I gave Cooper a rendezvous—is he going to come? Could he have confused the way? It's not probable. If he recoils? That's possible. The clown is like wolves and foxes. He only has courage at night. Ah! I had a moment of shame—it's when that man had me at his mercy and made me do what he wanted unable to think of anything—the sweat covered my face—It's hard to square his intelligence with the idiocy of these creatures who have nothing human about them but their shape! It's true that at the very moment when this inert bumpkin thought he was controlling me—it was I who manipulated him to my fancy—I can imagine his stupefaction when I tell him for what purpose I made him come. He's going to think I'm crazy—but luckily if he lacks intelligence, he doesn't lack pride and that's the way he must be caught. I'm mistaken. Gold is worth more than all that to decide a man. Love of gold—it's the source of all other passions since they can all be satisfied with gold! After having been the motivating force of the old world—gold has become that of the new. At the last judgment, what answer will all these souls give whose cupidity thrusts them into exile—when asked—what do you love on Earth? Gold—why did you leave your country? Gold! What did you hope for by crossing the seas? Gold! What was your faith? Gold! Always gold!

(listening)

Ah! I heard some steps—It's not him. Hola! Who goes—

(readying his rifle)

PAUL

(entering—putting himself on guard)

Who goes—yourself?

FULTON

Hunter—and you?

PAUL

Miner—your country?

FULTON

America—and yours?

PAUL

France—coming from—

FULTON

Melbourne—and you—?

PAUL

The mines.

FULTON

(extending his hand)

Then, friend.

PAUL

(tipping his hat)

Friend, so be it!

FULTON

(noticing that Paul hesitates to give him his hand)

You could dispense with saying you are French; I would have noticed.

PAUL

In England and America, sir—there's an excellent custom—it's not to shake hands with anyone before being presented.

FULTON

(bowing)

So be it! But as we have no one to present us, we must present ourselves. My name is Fulton, sir.

PAUL

Are you a descendent of the famous Fulton who invented the steamboat? In that case, you bear a great name. Genius surpasses nobility!

(Fulton bows)

And you hunt alone this way?

FULTON

I am with a companion who got separated—and I am waiting for him in this clearing—but you yourself—are you traveling alone?

PAUL

No, sir—I am with three companions.

FULTON

Three friends.

PAUL

Three associates—I am come first as scout.

FULTON

Scout?

PAUL

Yes, sir—we are coming from the mines and bearing the fruits of our labor to Melbourne.

FULTON

I thought there were a thousand men whose mission was to escort the miner's gold to Melbourne—and that thanks to this escort which watches over them.

PAUL

Sir, I don't know a mail coach more solid than a money belt, nor a surer escort than myself. There are four of us, well-armed—well resolved to defend ourselves. Soldiers, on the contrary, have no interest in defending these millions which don't belong to them—and turn their back at the first rifle shot. Anyway the roads are so bad that, leaving a day after the mail coach, we passed it two leagues from here and we will arrive at Melbourne five or six hours before it does.

(Mobile's voice can be heard.)

MOBILE

Ah, Marquis—where are you?

FULTON

Is it you they are calling, sir?

PAUL

I've forbidden them to call me that—but that's all they ever do

(going to the back)

Well—here I am—and so?

(Mobile, Catalin and Le Faucheux enter.)

MOBILE

Hey—you others—this way. Finally, there you are, Mr. Paul—I thought you had fallen in some ravine.

PAUL

(sitting to the right)

Not possible—there are only ditches.

MOBILE

Yes, but admit they are rough.

(cutting)

These are roads to get to paradise. In Paris, on the boulevard we have the macadam—but there's a depth in its place here. Ah, who would have said that I would regret my tax assessment—but who were you talking with there?

PAUL

With a hunter.

MOBILE

(low)

Of men. Is he alone?

PAUL

For the moment he's expecting a friend.

MOBILE

(raising his rifle)

Prudence is the mother of security.

(to Catalin and Le Faucheux)

Hey! You others.

VOICES OF CATALIN and LE FAUCHEUX

Here! Here!

FULTON

(to himself watching Mobile)

For certain, if that guy there had ever seen me—on the subject that concerns me—he will recognize me.

MOBILE

(to Paul)

Perhaps his companions are hereabouts and he is only there to give the signal.

PAUL

Well—as I'm not losing sight of him—at the moment he gives the signal I will send him a shot in the head.

MOBILE

(to Catalin and Le Faucheux)

Go get the horses. Buck up. In Melbourne they'll have a peck of oats and each of us a bottle of blue wine—which I yearn to taste before my departure—ah, the tasty vinegar—all that's missing are snails.

CATALIN

But while waiting if we ate a crust it's still a long trot from here to Melbourne.

LE FACHEUX

That is not seducing—biscuit—and as for liquid—sea water—and a hundred steps more.

FULTON

I have only a gourd full of Brandy—it's at your disposal.

MOBILE

My word—that's not to be refused.

(taking it)

PAUL

You are without manners, Mobile.

FULTON

Ah! Between travelers.

(laughing—to Paul)

You are not taking any, sir?

PAUL

Thanks.

FULTON

I beg you—

(Paul takes a handkerchief from his pocket and wraps the gourd in it.)

MOBILE

(watching him do it)

Get out! Right—that's the way one imbibes.

CATALIN

Only you've got to have a handkerchief—not everyone wears one.

LE FACHEUX

(pulling a rag from his pocket)

Who is it doesn't have a handkerchief?

MOBILE

Come, come—gang—the sun is setting. It's a question of not being too far behind it.

FULTON

You don't like to travel in darkness, sir?

MOBILE

No—I confess it—What I saw in the depths of the mines didn't give me limitless confidence in the night especially when the moon's forgotten to rise—Let's go, Mr. Paul.

PAUL

One minute! I have to confess I regret leaving this charming country without having found myself face to face with one of those redoubtable gold robbers—who are to cheaters what serpents are to beasts.

FULTON

(touching a pistol he wears at his belt)

You are brave—?

PAUL

More than they are cowards—for they only attack from the shadows—cringingly—

COOPER

(on a tree)

Ah—there, there—this is going to go wrong. I am annoyed to have come.

LE FAUCHEUX

(aside to Paul)

Mr. Paul—look at the face of the huntsman.

MOBILE

Come on, you others—let's sing the song of departure—that helps marching.

(singing)

No, no—no more traveling in this sad distant country.
Let's reach the shore.
While singing our song.
Long live—long live—France—
Land of beautiful weather.
Land of hope—
Land of love—

(they wave to Fulton and move away as the song ends)

FULTON

My compliments, gentleman.

COOPER

Are they gone?

FULTON

Yes—you see that plainly.

COOPER

I was afraid I'd arrived too soon.

FULTON

Why's that?

COOPER

Right. Didn't you recognize them?

FULTON

Indeed. They are miners from Ballarat. What's that to me? They didn't see me.

COOPER

Yes, but they saw me down there—

(hearing the singing—running to his tree)

I hear some noise. They're coming back.

FULTON

(listening)

No—it's the echo of their voices—they're moving off.

COOPER

It's all the same. The place isn't safe. Talk fast—I'm listening. What have we come here to do?

FULTON

What have we come here to do?

COOPER

Yes.

FULTON

You brought a pick axe?

FULTON

Where is it?

COOPER

There with the weapons.

FULTON

Well—to work then.

COOPER

To what work?

FULTON

Dig a trench.

COOPER

Where?

FULTON

At the foot of this tree.

COOPER

Why a trench?

FULTON

When are you going to be cured of your mania for asking questions? When I say dig a trench—dig a trench.

COOPER

(taking the pick)

Dig—dig—I have to execute my head to figure out your plan.

FULTON

(pointing to the foot of the tree)

There—dig—meanwhile I will tell you my plan. There's no time to lose.

COOPER

(digging)

I'm listening to you.

FULTON

You see, I'm tired of living the way I do. This life of a wild beast—hidden half the time in the forest—tires me.

COOPER

The fact is there's no comparison with the city.

FULTON

I warned you I was ambitious. What I want is a fortune—not by half—but immense, inexhaustible—well, tonight.

COOPER

Has fortune given you a meeting for tonight?

FULTON

Perhaps—and if it comes—I will be rich—with millions.

COOPER

And me?

FULTON

You, too—by God keep digging.

COOPER

Me, too? Heavens—don't tell me things like that—it breaks my arms and legs—and where might our millions be?

FULTON

A league—a half league—a quarter league—perhaps.

COOPER

You make me cold—in the back—good! Now I'm shivering from weakness—

FULTON

(giving him the gourd)

Warm yourself up.

COOPER

(drinking)

Ah—that's really good Brandy—good Brandy—that warms—

FULTON

My pick then.

COOPER

Ah! Pick yourself—now that I am warmed up—I want to know where our millions are.

FULTON

Where are they? They are in the mail coach carrying the gold.

COOPER

(releasing the pick)

In the mail coach carrying the gold? Are you mad?

FULTON

Why's that?

COOPER

And the escort?

FULTON

Six or eight men at most.

COOPER

Ah—you've found friends? It's a shame. Sharing adulterates the capital.

FULTON

There will be only two of us.

COOPER

You say? And with the two of us—we will stop—

FULTON

The escort and especially the one commanding it!

COOPER

Yes, yes—the fiancé of the little lady—it's your fixed idea to rid yourself of him—my poor Fulton—this is love—but as for me—I'm not in love and I find I can live comfortably with what I have already.

FULTON

Well—

COOPER

I wish you good luck and I'm going.

FULTON

(holding him)

Imbecile! When you've heard the way to have more gold—than you have ever—I won't say seen—but dreamed of—consider that you cannot make gold—but that with gold you can do everything—for my part—do you see—I believe myself in greater safety behind a wall of diamonds erected in broad daylight than in a fortress.

COOPER

Tempter!

FULTON

You are really ugly, my poor Cooper. Well, the prettiest woman on Earth will find you handsome and love you if you make a river of gold flow at her feet!

COOPER

A drop of Brandy, Fulton!

FULTON

(giving him the gourd)

Here, drink!

COOPER

It burns my heart! Look you were saying—?

FULTON

You understand clearly that we are not going to expose ourselves to a one-on-one struggle, right?

COOPER

(digging)

I understand absolutely nothing.

FULTON

(pointing to the distance)

Look at the road—it's crooked—worn down—carriages often get stuck in the mud for half a day. For us—it's worth four men! The coach that carries the gold has to pass through here. The moment you see the team of horses, kill the postilion's horse—the felled horse will kill the man.

COOPER

Kill! Kill! As for me, I don't like that. To take gold from a man won't kill him. But kill him—he never recovers from that.

FULTON

Pay attention to what I tell you. No injuries, deaths—no bravado—coolness—and I will answer for everything.

COOPER

(a bit drunk)

Ah—from the moment you answer for everything.

FULTON

If there are six of them, I'll take care of four myself.

COOPER

Fulton! Fulton! Leave us our skins!

FULTON

Do you think I don't cling to my skin as much as you do yours? It's newer. Listen, don't you hear something?

COOPER

Yes—I hear a storm coming, which is not going to spare our bones.

FULTON

What matter if we get wet—so long as our weapons don't get soaked!

COOPER

There— it's starting to fall.

FULTON

Do you hear?

COOPER

The thunder.

FULTON

No—the rumble of a carriage.

COOPER

Fulton—you will get us hanged!

FULTON

(giving him the gourd)

Here, drink. There are our millions! Are we going to let them pass us like nincompoops?

COOPER

(getting back in the tree)

You're going to see.

(Fulton hides behind a boulder)

(Storm, rain, lightning, thunder.)

WILLIAMS

(entering)

Great. Another ravine. Wait a second, I am going to explore the way.

(Cooper fires on Williams and misses)

FULTON

(to Tom Cooper)

Too soon.

WILLIAMS

(to his soldiers)

Dismount, my friends—and let's defend ourselves. Let's defend ourselves.

FULTON

You wanted a meeting with the Gold Robbers, sir? You've got your wish.

WILLIAMS

Mr. Fulton.

FULTON

Yes, Fulton—who hates you because he loves your fiancée.

WILLIAMS

Melida loves me enough that I have nothing to fear from any passion however great it may be. And still less that of a wretch and a coward! And it's not just a question of gold confided to my protection. I will leave you your life to prove to what degree I scorn you.

(fires at Fulton, but misses)

FULTON

You see less well then you said, sir—here I am forced to kill you.

(fires and wounds Williams)

WILLIAMS

Oh, the wretches! The cowards! My God! My men abandon me at the sight of trouble. I can no longer see the sky. I no longer feel the beating of my heart. Ah, Melida, Melida—we were not meant to be united in this world.

(he falls)

(Tom Cooper comes out of the tree and looks at Williams.)

FULTON

Well, what are you looking at him like that for?

COOPER

I am looking to see if he's done. Poor lad—his business is done. What are we going to do with all this gold here?

FULTON

Let's push everything in the ditch you made. Seeing the carriage stuck in the mud and the men dead—no one will have the idea to search so closely.

(he opens the trunk with the butt of his rifle and passes the bags to Cooper)

COOPER

What—it was to hide our gold that you made me dig this truck?

FULTON

Doubtless.

COOPER

You have a lot of confidence—such a fortune.

FULTON

I don't have confidence in a man, but in the ground.

COOPER

(recovering the sacks)

One cannot always be confident of the Earth.

FULTON

Come on—help me.

COOPER

(motionless looking at the gold as if stupefied)

I don't know if it's the brandy you made me drink—or the sight of the blood spread around me, but I don't feel well.

(looking at the gold which is at his feet)

And to say it's for this I sacrificed my health in this world and the next, ah—if it was to do over again—

FULTON

Decidedly, it's necessary that I finish with this man. There is not too much gold there for one! Still there's not enough for two.

(gives two sacks to Cooper)

COOPER

(letting one of the sacks fall beside the edge of the ditch)

Damn! I would never have thought I'd say carrying gold is too heavy.

FULTON

Well—why'd you let it fall?

COOPER

I'm going to pick it up, don't worry.

FULTON

(in the back)

Oh—Melida—you are not a woman—or you belong to me now.

COOPER

(letting the sack fall back)

I can't, I am tired.

FULTON

(arming a pistol and looking at Cooper)

You're tired? Well, take a rest.

(fires—Cooper falls by the ditch, face-down)

(pushing him into the ditch)

Guard my gold, Cooper. No one will come looking for it under your body. Let's go. Max is interred in the ditch with Cooper—greetings to the millionaire, Fulton!

(leaves on foot or horseback depending on the actor's riding ability)

COOPER

(emerging slowly)

Ah! Demon! You think me dead. You are mistaken. You cannot kill a man like me with a single shot. This wound makes me suffer horribly but I don't intend to die—no—I intend to avenge myself. Max! Max! We will see each other again!

(Williams utters a sigh. Cooper drags himself to him and places a hand on his head.)

Yes, this man is still living. Ah, Max, one of the two of us is going to insist on an account—perhaps the two of us.

CURTAIN

ACT IV

A salon in the Doctor's home. A big open window at the back through which can be seen a countryside.

LOUISA

(straightening up)

Well—how you gad about looking at the sky as if you were searching for a star in broad daylight.

PARISIAN

I am calming myself before addressing a word to you. I am calming myself.

LOUISA

You don't have that appearance—and the reason that requires you to assume this mortal calm?

PARISIAN

Say, reasons: I have a thousand.

LOUISA

Try to find a good one.

PARISIAN

You know them—since they come from you.

LOUISA

From me?

PARISIAN

You—who are making me quite simply die of shame.

LOUISA

Slow down—less fire?

PARISIAN

Less fire—naughty one—you are laughing.

LOUISA

(seriously)

No, you know that since the death of Mr. Williams, the devil's in this house—are you reproaching me for sympathizing with my benefactors—and yours?

PARISIAN

No, no—but we were engaged.

LOUISA

If you love me a little you must have some patience.

PARISIAN

It's because I love you that I don't have any at all.

LOUISA

How can we marry, be gay, happy, when everyone is in sadness, in tears?

PARISIAN

If you tell me such things—I will wait until the last judgment—but it's so long.

LOUISA

(offering her hand)

You know that we two are becoming one—my darling Parisian. The two of us have no country, riches, family—only our love.

PARISIAN

So, dear little wife, no news yet? The doctor's hopes.

LOUISA

(mysteriously)

Are very vague—but they hope—

PARISIAN

In whom, in what?

LOUISA

As all the searches made at Melbourne to retrieve the body of Mr. Williams have been in vain—the Doctor has charged Mr. Joanne.

PARISIAN

Mr. Joanne!

LOUISA

A young man whose life the doctor saved—well, he's charged him to make some searches in the mines.

PARISIAN

Ah, yes, I remember. Mr. Williams went to see him down there on behalf of the Doctor.

LOUISA

He's the same one! Well, he swore he will discover a clue, a track—hush!

(changing place)

He wrote—

PARISIAN

Why keep things so secret?

LOUISA

So as not to give false hopes to Miss Melida; then the people who killed him and made Mr. Williams disappear must be numerous and on the defense.

PARISIAN

They can kill and disappear Mr. Joanne.

LOUISA

Yes, and that would be a misfortune for you.

PARISIAN

For me?

LOUISA

Doubtless—under pretext of thanking the Doctor, Mr. Joanne came to see him often.

PARISIAN

You see—you never told me that.

LOUISA

(laughing)

In gratitude perhaps he loves Miss Émeraude.

PARISIAN

(breathing)

On—really!

LOUISA

He takes me for the sun and believes all the world admires me.

PARISIAN

Oh! I don't hide it. I am jealous of the moon when you walk without me—and that it looks at you with its big eyes.

LOUISA

Poor moon! What has it to do in all this?

PARISIAN

Nothing, it's true—since I cannot catch it—but him—

LOUISA

Ah—there's a him?

PARISIAN

My master's new coachman—a not so big thing who always rides by here.

LOUISA

If you weren't here so often you wouldn't see him.

PARISIAN

Yes, but I am on watch and I'm a good guard, I am.

LOUISA

You couldn't do everything.

PARISIAN

Possibly, I cannot do everything for my master—but when I am married. I don't want anybody's assistance, ah! But—

LOUISA

You are crazy! That big John doesn't say anything—and think no more about it.

PARISIAN

(aside)

Remains to be seen, remains to be seen.

MELIDA

(enters dressed in black; quietly, but profoundly sad)

Ah—it's you my friend.

PARISIAN

(presenting his bouquet)

Miss!

MELIDA

(taking the bouquet)

Always with a smile or flowers.

(placing the bouquet on the chimney)

I prefer his smile. Mr. Fulton overwhelms me. Doesn't he know that at this moment I only wish I was able to place them on a tomb?

PARISIAN

He's like us, Miss—he wants to distract you—make you forget a little.

MELIDA

Does he believe me capable of forgetting?— that's to believe me unworthy of wearing mourning for one whose memory will never be effaced from my heart. Inform my father that Mr. Joanne will be here in five minutes.

LOUISA

How sadly you say that, Miss! Perhaps Mr. Joanne is bringing you news of Mr. Williams.

MELIDA

If he brings some, he isn't bringing any good news—go.

LOUISA

What can you know?

MELIDA

Bearers of good news march more swiftly than Mr. Joanne is

marching at this moment—call my father, Louisa.

(Louisa leaves.)

PARISIAN

Hope, Miss—all our prayers are for you.

MELIDA

I know it—thanks.

(Parisian bows and leaves.)

MELIDA

(sitting at an armchair)

My God! My God! You test me beyond my strength.

DOCTOR

(entering quickly)

Tears in your eyes again. You make me despair.

MELIDA

(going to him and drying her eyes)

Father.

(she hugs him)

DOCTOR

Courage; a little resignation. I suffered what you are suffering when God took your poor mother from me, and I've lived for you. Live then for me. Dear soul of my soul, when I am no longer here, you will regret having made my last years so sad.

MELIDA

(kissing him)

Father!

DOCTOR

If death has taken from us, he who was full of strength, of youth and the future, why should it spare me? I no longer have anything to do in this world. See then how beautiful the sky is! At your age, you must despair of nothing.

MELIDA

(on her knees)

I love you, I love you. Oh, don't weep. You'll make me crazy—I love you.

DOCTOR

(pulling her into his arms)

That's it—fine—hold to each other; that will double our strength. You've seen Joanne?

MELIDA

I saw him from my window—seen everything down there. You see so far into the country!

DOCTOR

You guess what you don't yet see!

MELIDA

Yes—and I know in advance what they are going to tell me. Joanne, walking slowly head lowered—that's not the way one brings joy.

DOCTOR

(raising her up)

Your wit has been struck down by your heart. If you don't regain some confidence in the future—joy will never reenter your head—you frighten it off—

(Joanne enters)

Well?

JOANNE

(offering his hand to the Doctor)

I wanted to bring better news Doctor, though what I bring is no cause for despair.

DOCTOR

(to Melida)

You see!

MELIDA

I see excellent souls who are trying to console me a bit. You know my sorrow. To deceive me would perhaps be a pious lie, but I've just called up all my strength. I have the courage, the resignation—I want to know the truth—the whole truth.

JOANNE

I visited the place of the fight—I got information from those who brought away the dead, I consulted the investigative report. Nowhere is the death of Williams recorded.

DOCTOR

That's incredible—and I am lost in speculations.

MELIDA

If he wasn't dead, he would have written us, Father. Even in his own blood.

DOCTOR

That's true! Still they cannot have carried him off like a woman.

MELIDA

(putting her handkerchief to her eyes)

Everything is finished, go! God has abandoned me.

DOCTOR

This doubt is terrible—and however sad it may be, I would prefer a certitude.

MELIDA

Thanks, Joanne.

JOANNE

Wait—that's not all.

MELIDA

(standing—calm and sad)

You are trying to console me, Joanne, I can only say this to you—resigned, yes, consoled—never.

JOANNE

I extended my investigation further. As the sea isn't far from the place the attack occurred, I questioned the fisherman stationed on the shore.

DOCTOR

Well—

JOANNE

One of them almost assured me he'd seen during the night following the attack—two men—one slightly, the other gravely wounded. So gravely that he seemed dead. The one who was only slightly injured bargained with the owner of the biggest ship—so as to take his companion to land at Van Diemen.

DOCTOR

And what connection can that have with Williams? Those men were gold robbers taking flight so as not to be caught.

JOANNE

What do you want? In such circumstances, one grasps the least hope and if you like, well I will leave for Van Diemen to find the man who piloted this ship—and then in a month, you will have positive news.

MELIDA

Dear Joanne, you know quite well that Williams cannot be one of those two men—he had no motive to flee. In devoting yourself again you would waste your time—it's useless—go!—You wanted to take the most of my pain away—oh, my heart is broken, but it is not ungrateful. My sister loves you—she'll take care of discharging my debt of gratitude. As for me, I wasn't born to be happy. Right, father? Let destiny be accomplished! Thanks, Joanne, thanks.

(She leaves.)

JOANNE

(watching her leave)

Doctor, you'll believe me if you like—but I swear to you I'd give six years of my life to find Williams alive.

DOCTOR

Do you think I don't know that! My poor child! Her sadness makes me ill! To see her die of pain and to be able to do nothing.

JOANNE

Listen, it was so early in the morning when I crossed Melbourne, that I didn't dare present myself to the governor—but at this time, he must be up. He loved Williams—he's ordered active investigations. Perhaps he has discovered something. I don't know why but doubt refuses to enter my heart.

DOCTOR

I know it, my child; it's because Émeraude has made you happy with a word.

JOANNE

You call me "your child" Doctor?

DOCTOR

Joanne—know this—I will be half consoled the day I call you my son.

JOANNE

I want that to be soon. Ah! I am not egoist enough to think of myself. I'd be unworthy of you if I was that way. I'll get back on my horse and return to Melbourne. Are you going out today?

DOCTOR

I'm obliged to visit an American lady who lives a league from here.

JOANNE

Would you like me to leave you my horse?

DOCTOR

Thanks! Mr. Fulton has given me a ravishing little mare. Kitty.

JOANNE

You see this Mr. Fulton often?

DOCTOR

Almost every day.

JOANNE

So much the worse! I don't know him—I've never seen him—but they tell me he has the nerve to love Miss Melida—and I detest him.

ÉMERAUDE

(enters, hearing these last words)

Good—yet another one! If that's your opinion, Mr. Joanne, at least don't speak too loud!

DOCTOR

My dear Joanne—know once and for all the Émeraude has set herself up as Mr. Fulton's defender: She adores him.

ÉMERAUDE

Why I am grateful to him. We are living in an agreeable way and we owe it to him. Truly, one would say he unearths patients to give you clients.

DOCTOR

Unearths patients! Dear child, don't say things like that in front of a doctor!

ÉMERAUDE

I'm not joking—it desolates me that everybody seems to hate a man that I regard as our benefactor! He loved Melida before the arrival of poor Williams—he didn't know him.

DOCTOR

(with dignity)

You've mistaken—no one here hates Fulton. And me in particular, I have sympathy of him—but that doesn't go so far as to wish to force Melida's inclinations. Let Mr. Fulton do what Joanne is doing—let him take time. Time leads sometimes too quickly to forgetfulness. Go, Joanne, go!

(Joanne starts to leave and returns)

JOANNE

(taking Émeraude's hand)

You are right. If he sincerely loves your sister he must suffer—and I am becoming your ally. Later.

ÉMERAUDE

God protect you: Later.

(Exit Joanne.)

DOCTOR

Dear child—hurry my lunch and order them to feed Kitty oats. She's your protégée—she comes from Mr. Fulton. Well! Double her rations—go.

ÉMERAUDE

Yes, father.

DOCTOR

With what an air you say that—there's no happiness except for you here—and you seem sad.

ÉMERAUDE

It's because you don't hug me father.

DOCTOR

Great! There you are jealous of your sister?

ÉMERAUDE

No—but—

DOCTOR

No, but you must have your share of affection, like a flower its share of the sun. As for you, you are my strength, Melida, my weakness—but I love you each equally—go.

(he hugs her)

(the girl goes out)

Poor child—she sees only one thing—the misery which we have so miraculously escaped—and which she fears falling back into—not for herself—the saintly creature—but for me. Oh! This cursed country: land of exile, regrets, deceptions—if I had known.

LOUISA

(enters—announcing)

Mr. Fulton.

DOCTOR

Show him in—show him in! He knows very well he is at home here.

FULTON

(entering)

Thanks, Doctor, but you know my character, I doubt myself.

DOCTOR

Not at all—you're wrong to do that.

FULTON

Are you giving me a word of hope, Doctor?

DOCTOR

Are you so ill that I must deceive you and tell you yes?

FULTON

No—today—I prepared myself. I feel almost strong—and can stand anything. Melida?

DOCTOR

Melida is not yet beyond gratitude, my dear Fulton—the rest will come perhaps—but it requires time and patience.

FULTON

That's easy for you to say. You are not in love! I go crazy when I meet a difficulty! You told me one day that love is an illness—which can be treated like other maladies of the heart. Well—if you spoke the truth—I abandon myself to you—cure me for I am ill to death.

DOCTOR

You are mad!

FULTON

I just told you so myself.

DOCTOR

(reflecting)

What can I do for you?

FULTON

Kill me or cure me—I prefer death to this illness. Miss Melida flees me—if she sees me coming she leaves the room. If I meet her with her sister—she clings to her. If I surprise her alone—and surprise is the correct word—she calls—is that the result of bad luck for me? I hope so.

(Melida enters.)

FULTON

Indeed, since I've come to your home dear, Doctor, I haven't been able to exchange a single word which hasn't been criticized by a third party—this ought to render me clumsy and unoriginal.

(Melida hears the last words.)

FULTON

Well, Doctor, arrange an interview with Miss Melida—so I can express my feelings to her—I know hers—she hates me so.

DOCTOR

She hates you so.

FULTON

I will leave Melbourne—I am rich—the Earth is large—finally, let me see her—let me speak to her—I beg you.

MELIDA

You wish to speak to me, sir—here I am.

DOCTOR

You see—she's coming herself as you wished. Whatever happens know her inclination from her frank candor. As for me, I have no other will than hers.

MELIDA

You're leaving, Father?

DOCTOR

Yes—I have a visit to make—I will return in an hour—Kitty travels fast.

MELIDA

Take care you don't have an accident with that horse you hardly know.

FULTON

(interrupting her)

Ah—don't be afraid. I've ridden her a hundred times.

MELIDA

You, sir, are a good horseman, while my father—

DOCTOR

Rides horses like a good country curate, right? And I had pretensions. Well, you shall watch me leave, Miss—I am going to go at a gallop to return the quicker.

MELIDA

Be prudent.

FULTON

That mare has only one fault—

DOCTOR

Gratitude—she cannot forget the way which leads to your house. Imagine dear child, that the other day, I had left her tied to the door at the home of a patient, I was visiting—

FULTON

And she had the factiousness to break her tether and run to my home at a fast gallop—I had to correct her.

MELIDA

I regret it, sir, for it doesn't do honor to your memory. For the day on which she brought you here for the first time, this mare saved your life by receiving the shot in her breast which was intended for you.

DOCTOR

Everybody's crazy about Kitty, as for me, I do whatever she wishes and I prefer to let her escort me to China than to give her a blow with the crop. She's so fine a horse when she's good.

(Exit Doctor.)

MELIDA

We are alone, sir—speak, I am listening to you.

FULTON

Don't you know all that I have to tell you? And aren't taking an evil pleasure in freezing on my lips the burning protests trying to escape my heart? With your frigid glance!

MELIDA

I know, sir, that you have done me the honor of noticing me.

FULTON

Then you know that I love you—and I'm going crazy. Yes, mad—is the only word which describes the feeling I have for you. Yes, mad desire! Delirium which consumes me, which carries me away despite myself—despite the obstacles, the dangers. I vainly ask myself why I love you—you who avoid me, hate me perhaps.

MELIDA

You are right. An explanation has become indispensable. Listen to me then with all your patience—sir, and don't interpret my words ill.

(she makes a sign for Fulton to take a chair and sit near her)

FULTON

Speak, speak, I hear you with my heart.

MELIDA

(sitting down)

Listen with your mind, sir. For there are sad and serious things I have to tell you. You know that I was Williams' fiancée! You know that I loved him.

(Fulton makes an affirmative sign)

But what you don't know is that I love him still!

FULTON

I am not jealous of the dead!

MELIDA

Everyone tells me that without consideration, without pity—but no one proves it to me.

FULTON

His silence—

MELIDA

Perhaps—independent of his will—if he were prisoner.

FULTON

Gold robbers never do that sort of thing. Where would they put them when they were wandering or pursued?

MELIDA

That's true.

FULTON

Your enemy rather than your friend would let your heart nourish such vain chimeras.

MELIDA

Chimeras perhaps, but what do you want? The loving heart clings to the most futile hopes!

FULTON

I thought you were convinced from seeing you wear mourning like a widow.

MELIDA

Isn't absence a sort of half death? But what do you want? Until his body is found, until his cadaver shall have told me through his gaping wounds: "No more hope! All is finished!" I shall take refuge in the grandeur, the goodness, the mercy of God!

FULTON

God! God doesn't give eternal life! Your Williams is dead!

MELIDA

(rising and looking in his face)

What do you know about it?

FULTON

He is dead and you will forget him.

MELIDA

Never—wait—a strange thing is happening in me when they try to console me with these banal words which have no effect on deeply sincere hearts! Instead of consoling me—they make me despair—but far from weakening the doubt which trembles in my heart—this doubt grows—becomes a type of hope—and I say to myself—no, Williams is not dead.

FULTON

Wish that that not be true, Melida—for if it were, Melida, if Williams were not dead—if he returned—

MELIDA

If he returned—

FULTON

I would kill him.

MELIDA

Take care, sir, take care what you say—suspicion gives birth to ideas, suspicions so strange they mustn't be tested.

FULTON

I am weary of suffering! I am jealous of the past, of the present, of the future! Your disdain irritates—can you make me commit the crime of loving you too much?

MELIDA

I can only pity you.

(goes off a little.)

FULTON

Yes, by tearing from me all my illusions, all my hopes.

MELIDA

Have I ever given you any? Look, sir, you are young, you are rich—the world is yours—as they say—for with gold you can buy the world! You have the choice of all the women in Melbourne—who will you choose? A poor pale complexioned creature with eyes red from tears, with a broken heart—not only do you say to her—" Here I am—love me!" But worse, "You've loved another for 10 years, this man has vanished for six weeks—"

FULTON

(somberly)

He's dead!

MELIDA

(looking at him)

So be it, he is dead—

FULTON

I will tear from your heart his memory—all his memory and give me his place!

MELIDA

Impossible!

FULTON

To all this I can answer only one thing: I love you like a maniac; I know that is the language of an egoist! But it's useless to suffer. You don't want to admit defeat! Melida—judge my suffering from yours—my soul struggles. It twists in the grasp of jealousy—Melida—I can renounce the world, fortune, life—but you never—

MELIDA

You've just pronounced your sentence, sir! If you affirm you can never forget me—you who hardly know me, how can you expect I will forget Williams?

(She leaves.)

FULTON

(watching her leave)

Ah, Melida! This love will bring me misfortune! But were it to cost me my life, you will be mine.

ÉMERAUDE

(entering)

Ah, my God, Mr. Fulton, what's wrong?

FULTON

Wrong—wrong—I'm the most wretched of men.

ÉMERAUDE

Come on! Come on! You mustn't despair this way. Time makes all forget, I had like you—a disappointed passion in which I had entombed the future. The one I loved was not dead—he had married another. Well, sadness succeeded despair—melancholy, sadness—finally forgetfulness to melancholy. Give time a chance—why won't it work a miracle for Mr. Fulton as it did for Joanne?

FULTON

(excitedly)

Joanne, you say?

ÉMERAUDE

Yes, a poor young man that my father saved in the mines—you know him.

FULTON

I knew—but perhaps he's not the same?

ÉMERAUDE

If you had come a quarter of an hour sooner, you would have been able to see for yourself.

FULTON

He's here?

ÉMERAUDE

He was here this morning—he will be here in an hour. He's in Melbourne investigating for us and for himself.

FULTON

For himself!

ÉMERAUDE

Yes, he's sworn to avenge the death of his friend, Albert! He knows the author of the crime. They met at sea.

FULTON

(frightened)

At sea.

(Louisa enters.)

FULTON

(aside)

Joanne, Joanne in this house—Hell is meddling in this.

ÉMERAUDE

I'm going to go ahead to meet him on the road. I am late being happy—and I want to make up for lost time. Your turn will come—courage.

(Exit Émeraude.)

FULTON

(without listening to her)

Joanne here! I am lost if he sees me.

(writing a few words on a paper)

Yes—all for all—ruin for ruin—John! John!

JOHN

(entering)

Sir—

FULTON

(giving the paper to him)

Listen to me carefully, John, when I toss this bouquet out this window—you will read this.

JOHN

When you throw this bouquet, I will read it.

FULTON

You are intelligent, John. If you execute my orders carefully in the next hour I will give you three years' wages.

(John exits.)

My course is decided.

(he looks at his pistol which he hurriedly hides in his pocket as he sees Melida enter)

MELIDA

(entering)

I heard you speak; I thought my father had returned.

FULTON

I was waiting for him to take my leave of him—Miss—and say my goodbyes to him.

MELIDA

(joyfully)

You are leaving.

FULTON

Yes, I've understood that my presence would be a burden to you and that I wouldn't have the courage to spare you if I remained in this country! I'm going to leave Melbourne for a long time—perhaps forever—if I do that, shall I be able to count on your esteem—on your affection?

MELIDA

You have that of all my family.

FULTON

I am going to leave you making you a vow! And believe that it costs me much in terms of strength—still, I am sincere. I want your hope to be realized that Williams despite all expectations may not be dead—that the investigations that Mr. Joanne is making have a lucky result—so that the one you love will return to give you the happiness which I cannot.

(he bows and starts to leave)

MELIDA

(crossing)

May God hear you.

FULTON

Promise to think of me sometimes and if the one you love is dead and someday—

MELIDA

Sir!

FULTON

No! No! I am mad—forget me completely—let nothing, not even a word, not even a flower recall me to you—poor flowers—you don't look at them.

(taking the bouquet and throwing it out the window)

Go—fade and die—since there's not a drop of water here to refresh your stems.

MELIDA

(softly)

I had forgotten them—pardon me.

FULTON

I pardon you for all I have suffered and all I am going to suffer far from you.

JOHN

(enters quickly)

Mr. Fulton! Mr. Fulton!

FULTON

What's wrong—and who let you in this way?

JOHN

A great misfortune, Mr. Fulton!

FULTON

(rushing to him)

A misfortune.

JOHN

(lowering his voice but in a way that Melida can still hear)

The Doctor was carried by your mare.

FULTON

The cursed beast will have gone to my house—it refuses to forget its stable.

JOHN

The Doctor fell and they say he has a broken leg.

FULTON

Speak lower, wretch!

MELIDA

(rushing)

What's this man say?

FULTON

Nothing—nothing—he talking about someone you don't know.

MELIDA

You want to deceive me—I heard the name of my father.

FULTON

But perhaps it's less grave than they say. I have my coach and I'm going.

MELIDA

(taking a cloak)

I am going with you.

FULTON

Inform Miss Émeraude.

JOHN

She's not here. I saw her leave a long while ago.

(He leaves.)

FULTON

That's true. She went ahead for Mr. Joanne.

MELIDA

I will go alone! Ah, come, sir—I am dying of anxiety.

FULTON

(bowing and offering her his arm)

I indeed said she would be mine.

(They leave.)

(Louisa enters and watches them leave.)

LOUISA

Miss is leaving with Mr. Fulton—she who always avoided him—was Miss Émeraude, right? There she goes in the carriage with him—if I hadn't seen it myself—

ÉMERAUDE

(entering)

You wouldn't believe it. Me either. But I saw him with both my eyes—saw poor sister going to be happy—it's necessary to tell her gently.

LOUISA

(who has remained near the window)

Tell who, Miss?

ÉMERAUDE

Williams is following me.

WILLIAMS

(entering with Joanne)

And very closely—hello my good Louisa.

ÉMERAUDE

Tell Melida.

LOUISA

Yes, run—yes, I—

(aside)

What to do—I don't dare say she left with Mr. Fulton—let's try to gain time.

WILLIAMS

Ah—minutes are centuries for me, Joanne! Oh, my poor Joanne! How quickly misfortune is forgotten when one is happy—illness, suffering privations—I've forgotten all them crossing the sill of this door.

ÉMERAUDE

To be living and not to have given us news—

WILLIAMS

Because I was living and dead at the same time, my good sister—one of the bandits who attacked the escort had pity on me. I'd fainted—wounded. He had me placed on a ship that left for Van Diemen.

JOANNE

The thief was afraid to be compromised transporting his prisoner.

WILLIAMS

Don't speak ill of him—he could have finished me. I was at sea and I couldn't send news—but hardly had I touched land than I took flight—I re-embarked and here I am—forgetting until now the pain of a wound which almost deprived me of the happiness of seeing you again.

ÉMERAUDE

(calling)

Melida! Melida!

LOUISA

(entering)

She isn't there, Miss.

ÉMERAUDE

Ah—where is she?

LOUISA

(low)

She left with Mr. Fulton.

ÉMERAUDE

That's impossible.

WILLIAMS

If this Fulton is the one I saw here on the day of my arrival—he's the same one I met in the forest—he's the leader of the gold thieves—my murderer.

JOANNE

(entering)

I saw a man leaving this house by this side. I thought I recognized him—Max or Fulton. He's the same. Oh! Melida, Melida.

WILLIAMS

You saw him leave? Lead us and bad luck to him.

JOANNE

Oh—if you knew how she loves you—!

WILLIAMS

You give me back hope!

(to Émeraude)

We will bring her back to you, my sister, or the two of us will die defending her.

CURTAIN

ACT V

A room in Fulton's house. A large window at the back decorated with large curtains which are open and give on a balcony overlooking the sea. To the right an armoire with secret drawers—doors to the left and right—chairs and armchairs.

At rise, Tom Cooper enters surreptitiously and listens.

COOPER

Those two men have lost my track. What the devil could they want from me?

(looking out the window)

I'm not mistaken—one of the two is rowing a canoe under the balcony and the other one is preparing to climb up. Thieves without doubt. Let's try to find out.

(Cooper leaves carefully the way he came. A the same moment, Le Faucheux's head appears above the balcony which he climbs over. He makes a quick tour of the room—opens the door at the left then makes an owl's cry. Catalin responds.)

CATALIN

(coming over the balcony)

If they heard us they'll be pretty surprised.

LE FAUCHEUX

Surprised by what?

CATALIN

Hearing the songs of night owls in the plain day.

LE FAUCHEUX

Bah! No one will be taking any precautions—in this extravagant country everything seems natural. And the boat?

CATALIN

Solidly tied to the bottom of the stairway leading here.

(pointing to the door at the left)

It's time we had an explanation. You said to me "Come with me—I'm on the track of some game which is worth its weight in gold." I replied "I am your man. Where must we go? What must we do?" You told me "Follow me without asking questions. You'll know everything when we get there."

LE FAUCHEUX

(mysteriously)

Yes—here's the pavilion.

CATALIN

It seems inhabited to me—do you intend to rent it—to offer me room and board?

LE FAUCHEUX

(sighing)

To rent a pavilion of this sort you'd have to be richer than we are.

CATALIN

It's you who made me eat up my money. Ah! If I'd listened to Paul and Mobile I'd have returned to France with them.

LE FAUCHEUX

No risk—no gain. We've lost everything at cards but we're going to double our capital.

CATALIN

(pulling out a sack from his pocket)

Meanwhile—here's all that remains to us—! A pouch which would be filled with tobacco—if we had enough to buy some to fill it.

LE FAUCHEUX

I promised you to fill it.

CATALIN

With tobacco?

LE FAUCHEUX

(mysteriously)

No—gold. The government has posted at the mine a reward of 1,000 pounds sterling to whoever delivers up a gold robber—I've discovered one—he's hiding here—and one has the right to nab them at home since you cannot knock down the doors.

CATALIN

You entered by way of the window—but are you sure—?

LE FAUCHEUX

Yes—he's one of those who killed that poor Albert.

CATALIN

Ah! Ah! The Bandit—if you can put my hand on him, I won't have any scruples.

LE FAUCHEUX

Especially if you pull your hand out with five hundred sterling—

CATALIN

Hell! I confess that with what I have—

LE FAUCHEUX

(laughing)

You'll have five hundred pounds. Yesterday, I was on the lookout—I saw my man heading this way—he went to ground here—but he noticed me and disappeared as if the devil were carrying him off—

(looking out the window)

Hey, do you see the boat down there—that's moving off?

CATALIN

Yes.

LE FAUCHEUX

That must be him; he must have seen or heard us—come, he mustn't escape us this time.

CATALIN

(loading his rifle)

Do we have the right to injure them a bit?

LE FAUCHEUX

By God, you can blow 'em to pieces!

(They leave.)

COOPER

(entering)

Ah—if it wouldn't make too much noise, I would put a bullet in each of those guys! Ah, they are full of good will toward me—but they don't know who they are dealing with. I made a pile of branches and dressed it in my cloak and put in the boat which I untied—I hoisted the sail and I put it to the wind which is driving it adrift—they're going to follow it.

(looking out the window)

I'm not mistaken—there the road begins—and before they notice they've been hoaxed, I'll have time to settle my business here—ah, if this Williams that I saved hadn't abandoned me—what a fine vengeance I would offer him today. Anyway, my strength has come back. I will act alone. I've delayed too long asking for my score—friend Max—; I promised to return what you gave me and I'm going to pay you completely—capital and interest. Here's our hiding place. You will come by way of the land.

(points right)

And you'll leave by the way of the sea.

(goes and opens the door)

Here's a stairway leading to the door which gives on the sea—at the foot—a canoe—in case of need. That's good to know.

(returning)

At last—it's him—the Devil—he's not alone. Well—bad luck to those who get between him and me.

(checking his pistol)

No—indeed—no compromises.

(goes out)

(Fulton and Melida enter.)

FULTON

Pardon for having made you get down in a carriage so far from the house, but it is impossible to get here in a carriage

MELIDA

You are completely excused, sir—your horse devoured the space, but it seems to me I would have been even faster on foot.

(looking at Fulton, who closes the door by which they entered)

Where is my father?

FULTON

In this pavilion.

MELIDA

Seconds seem like days to me.

(looking at Fulton uneasily)

This house seems inhabited. How did my father get in, since you have the key—let's hurry, I'm dying of anxiety.

FULTON

(laughing)

There are two entrances. You can't hide your aversion from me—there you are all shivering.

(he tries to take her hand)

MELIDA

(withdrawing her hand)

I'm feverish with impatience.

FULTON

Because you are alone with me—Oh! Quite alone.

MELIDA

(trying to compose herself)

What have I to fear? You are the friend of my family.

FULTON

I am a man who loves you more than his life.

MELIDA

Sir, the moment is ill chosen to speak to me—

FULTON

—of love that you disdain—but it must share a day—

MELIDA

(aside)

Oh, my God! I have been aware of nothing. How did I get here? Of my own will—no one forced me. What interest would John have to deceive me?

(with fright)

Sir, I want to see my father, I—

(Fulton laughs)

Sir, mercy—don't oblige me to doubt my sanity—or yours.

FULTON

I lost mine the day I saw you for the first time—if you loved me, you would have followed me of your own free will—you didn't want to. I kidnapped you.

MELIDA

Kidnapped! How could you have abused my confidence and my sorrow?

FULTON

In love as in war—all means are good.

MELIDA

I can scream—call for help.

FULTON

No one will come.

MELIDA

I must be the victim of a bad dream—and if I thought it was real, I would pity you for telling me you are mad—

FULTON

(mocking)

Is pity the only feeling I can inspire in you?

MELIDA

Yes—and deep pity for in an hour, you will repent—a moment of passion has led you astray. You've taken me for an ordinary woman who gives in to fear—you're mistaken. Danger increases my courage. Threats leave me impassive—if need be I can chose death over shame.

FULTON

If you are not an ordinary woman, neither am I an ordinary man. I've told myself that at whatever price I would be rich and powerful. You are in my power, I am rich enough to pay for your love.

MELIDA

(controlling herself)

Ah, sir—were you the last man on Earth—when one loves a woman, one does not insult her. Here, open this door. Release me—let me go—and I will pardon you—I will do more—I will forgive you.

FULTON

You're a mad woman. Why you don't realize that to see you each day, each hour, each moment, I risked my liberty, my head—I conquered men—I achieved a fortune—I know how to master a woman.

MELIDA

Open that door and I will believe that you love me.

FULTON

Why you ask more than my life. I love you.

MELIDA

I despise you.

FULTON

Take care—you see—I am not accustomed to beg. By humiliating me—you break my heart—take care. One word—I will repent of the past—I will become good in the future—I'll purify this soul which gives itself to you in its entirety. I love you.

MELIDA

My God! Have you abandoned me?

FULTON

(at the back)

No—since He sends you fortune.

(taking papers)

In this envelope there's a million in bank notes—In this armoire—

(touching a spring)

There's enough gold to blind you.

(showing his gold to Melida)

All this is yours.

MELIDA

The sight of gold doesn't fascinate me and were it a thousand times more it wouldn't diminish the horror you inspire in me.

FULTON

(throwing the gold with rage)

Why think, wretched woman, that Max breaks whatever refuses to bend before him!

MELIDA

Max—your name is Max? You are the murderer of Joanne and Albert?

FULTON

(recoiling)

Who told you that?

MELIDA

(looking him in the face)

The memory of a shadow I saw at the mines—my invincible aversion for you—and finally your pallor.

FULTON

I've betrayed myself. Well! Well! If that were true—do you tremble?

MELIDA

(energetically)

No! For I would tell myself that such a man understands I can never love him—he will kill me in fear that I will denounce him—which I will do—if I leave here with any breath remaining.

FULTON

Then you don't fear death?

MELIDA

Not when it appears to me in the shape of deliverance.

FULTON

Melida—I beg you—look, I have tears in my eyes, the first in my life—if you knew what I've suffered since I've loved you. I must have expiated all my sins—do you know pity?

MELIDA

Pity halts before God's justice.

WILLIAMS

(in the distance)

Doctor! Joanne! This way! This way!

MELIDA

Did you hear? It's Williams' voice.

(running to the window)

Ah, my God—they're going away—Father! Williams!

FULTON

(looking in his turn and preventing her from screaming)

Williams, Ah! Yes—you spoke the truth—you've just pronounced the judgment of death on both of them.

MELIDA

(coming to herself)

Ah! I'm not afraid of you anymore now.

FULTON

(taking her hand)

Fool! Don't attempt a struggle in which I can break you to pieces. Rather than give you up to the one I detest more than I love you, I will kill you twenty times.

(making Melida fall to her knees)

MELIDA

Oh, the coward—he doesn't kill his victims—he tortures them.

(twisting free and running to the window)

Help!

FULTON

(seizing her and pushing her again to the left)

Shut up or I won't answer for myself.

COOPER

(rushing between them)

Well, touch her if you dare.

FULTON

(recoiling)

Cooper!

COOPER

I told you that I killed a man because he beat a woman in front of me. Well, if I were to hear this young girl scream again, I could begin all over.

FULTON

(raging)

Ah! Death rejects those I send him?

COOPER

Still, you put them there with perseverance and good will!

FULTON

(arming a pistol)

You've figured me out, demon; but this time you won't escape.

COOPER

(calmly)

There are a lot of people around this pavilion and if they hear a detonation that might attract the curious. Don't do stupid things—you have too much passion in business—you get carried away so far that you over reach.

FULTON

(recoiling and disarming his pistol)

It seems he dominates me in his turn. Heavens, Cooper—I repent!

COOPER

Of not having done more ill to your poor familiar brother?

FULTON

I'm in love and love purifies all.

COOPER

That it doesn't debase.

FULTON

(running to the armoire)

Here, Cooper—see this gold—these riches—they are yours—if you will help me carry off this woman.

COOPER

(dazzled)

All that to carry her off by the little stairway which goes down to the sea?

(he runs to Melida as if to seize her. She recoils, terrified.)

MELIDA

Ah! I am lost!

COOPER

(very quickly)

Don't be so frightened—you've run a long race. A canoe is waiting for you. You sit to the rear—you take the oar in one hand, the sail in the other and with the grace of God—

(he reveals the door)

MELIDA

(looking at him)

Ah—I understand.

(Fulton is taking paper money and gold from the armoire.)

COOPER

(opening the door)

Leave—hurry up.

MELIDA

(leaving)

But he's going to kill you.

COOPER

(pushing her out)

Oh, he's really capable of that. If he succeeds—you will pray to God for me.

(locking the door)

If that doesn't do any good, it can't do any harm.

(he leans on the door)

FULTON

(turning)

Why, she's escaping me.

COOPER

Heavens—so stupid—since I made her scamper off.

FULTON

What—you dared—?

COOPER

(jokingly)

Ah, my God, yes, and I'm going to dare much more.

FULTON

Allow me to pass.

COOPER

Why no—we'll start over the scene you were playing with the little kid; she interested me—that young girl—and since I was so lucky as to rescue her from your claws and save her lover—well, they will rejoice—I intend that those kids be happy.

FULTON

Tom Cooper, you are driving me mad. Let me pass or I will annihilate you.

COOPER

Big words and airs. You shan't pass and you won't annihilate anybody. Just now you were hurting an innocent creature without power or defense. Try breaking the bones of this fist or look too near these arms. When I submitted to your domination, I took you for a lion. You are only a jackal.

FULTON

You've discovered this and you're not afraid?

COOPER

No—because I regard you with scorn, because you've made me ashamed of the past and disgusted with the future. You lied to me when you said you could buy everything with gold. There was enough there to pay for an angel's fall and this poor creature preferred martyrdom—you see that plainly. Honest conscience cannot be bought.

FULTON

(looking through the window on the left)

She's going off but another skiff is joining her—Williams is doubtless there; well, he will arrive too late.

(firing three shots in Melida's direction)

Got her; not me—then no one else!

COOPER

(rushing and pushing him to the left)

Wretch!

(looking out to sea)

Poor creature—she's folded up like a bird under the wing. Dead, without doubt.

(he lowers his eyes)

FULTON

(holding his head in despair)

Oh cursed—cursed me—it's you who came here to throw yourself between us—; without you, she would still be living. Ah, Melida, Melida.

COOPER

Good! He's going to weep now.

FULTON

(furious, coming to himself)

No, but to avenge her!

(wants to strike Tom Cooper)

COOPER

(recoiling and parrying the blow)

On me—that's not natural!

(they wrestle, separate and go to it again. Cooper parries the blow and strikes Fulton—he picks him up and drags him to the balcony to throw him into the sea, but hearing a voice, he places Fulton on the balcony—closes the curtains and escapes by the door on the left.

JOANNE

(entering, looking around)

Over here. Over here.

(brings an armchair forward)

Williams.

(enters carrying Melida)

Oh—Father, this fainting spell resembles death.

DOCTOR

(to Melida who's been placed on the arm chair)

Melida, my child, answer me.

WILLIAMS

(on his knees)

Her hands are cold— she no longer hears me—Melida.

MELIDA

(opening her eyes)

Williams—Father! Oh—this house!

DOCTOR

Wretched child! What a fright you gave us!

MELIDA

Ah, don't scold me, Father, if you knew what I suffered these last two hours—leaving this pavilion, I threw myself in a boat which moved away with a mortal slowness—when a bullet cut through the small sail—that I never took my eyes off—from fear or by instinct of self-preservation, I lay down in the canoe—several other bullets whistled over my heard. The wind rose suddenly and carried me away with terrifying speed. I lost consciousness.

WILLIAMS

You were going to founder on the reefs without a doubt when I saw you; I had been searching for you with my heart. Ah, this time we will never leave each other again—we will hold each other so close that the shade of misfortune will never find a place between us. Come.

COOPER

(returning by the left with Le Faucheux and Catalin, who aim at him)

Why, you've got the devil in you to pursue me like this.

LE FAUCHEUX

I've got the devil in my rifle. Don't budge or I let the dog loose.

COOPER

Look, what do you want with me?

CATALIN

To sell your hide.

COOPER

Sell my hide to who?

LE FAUCHEUX

To the government.

COOPER

What's the government got to do with it?

CATALIN

They'll tell you at the courthouse. Come on, let's get going—by way of the gallows road.

WILLIAMS

(to the Doctor)

Father, this man saved my life; I owe him the happiness of seeing you again.

MELIDA

If they take this unfortunate man, it's death for him—think that he not only saved my life, he saved my honor.

COOPER

(who's come forward)

Yes, and to reward me, she's placed the rope around my neck with her pretty little hands.

DOCTOR

I don't understand.

COOPER

It's quite simple—I made her embark on the boat I could have used to save myself and because I don't walk on water, I was nabbed by these fine gentlemen.

CATALIN

Come, come—let's be on our way.

DOCTOR

(signaling to Cooper to approach)

Stop—we owe you a great deal, sir.

COOPER

(taking his hat off)

Ah—I ask for nothing.

DOCTOR

(low)

Not even your freedom on a simple promise to change your way of life?

COOPER

(beaten)

Life, oh! I've seen it ready to escape me so often that I no longer cling to it—

DOCTOR

You can pay for wrongs by good acts.

COOPER

You think that's possible?

DOCTOR

Yes, since you've already begun.

COOPER

(coming to himself)

Well—as surely as you are a brave and honest man, I will try to end well.

DOCTOR

(to Catalin)

I will answer for this man, he belongs to me.

COOPER

(to Doctor)

Yes—body and soul.

WILLIAMS

(low to Cooper)

Where is your accomplice?

COOPER

Max, why you are standing where I killed him.

(suddenly the curtains open and Fulton appears—covered with blood—then advances—staggering)

FULTON

Killed me, yes, you've killed me, Cooper—I don't wish you ill for it. Justice was done.

(still coming forward)

Melida—you didn't want my love—well, I give you my life—

(he falls dead)

CATALIN

And our reward?

JOANNE

(pointing to Fulton)

You were looking for Max—the murderer of Albert—there he is.

WILLIAMS

(pointing to Fulton)

You were looking for Fulton—the leader of the gold robbers—there he is.

CURTAIN

ABOUT THE AUTHOR

Frank J. Morlock has written and translated many plays since retiring from the legal profession in 1992. His translations have also appeared on Project Gutenberg, the Alexandre Dumas Père web page, Literature in the Age of Napoléon, Infinite Artistries.com, and Munsey's (formerly Blackmask). In 2006 he received an award from the North American Jules Verne Society for his translations of Verne's plays. He lives and works in México.

www.ingramcontent.com/pod-product-compliance
Lightning Source LLC
LaVergne TN
LVHW040115080426
835507LV00039B/258